# FOR WHOM THE BELL TOLLS

ERNEST HEMINGWAY

No man is an *Iland*, intire of it selfe; every man is a peece of the *Continent*, a part of the *maine*; if a *Clod* bee washed away by the *Sea*, *Europe* is the lesse, as well as if a *Promontorie* were, as well as if a *Mannor* of thy *friends* or of *thine owne* were; any mans *death* diminishes *me*, because I am involved in *Mankinde*; And therefore never send to know for whom the *bell* tolls; It tolls for *thee*

JOHN DONNE

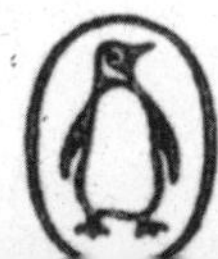

# *The Modern World*

## *II*

## *Realities*

# THE MODERN WORLD ENCYCLOPÆDIA

## Vol. VI

## Land to Obelisk

# THE MODERN WORLD ENCYCLOPÆDIA

VOL. I

A TO BED

# THE OXFORD BOOK OF DREAMS

CHOSE[illegible]

S[illegible]OK

Oxford New York

# *The Modern World*

## *III*

## *Reactions*

# *The Modern World*

## *I*

## *Hopes*

# THE MISMEASURE OF MAN

*Stephen Jay Gould*

'If the misery of our poor be caused not by the laws of nature, but by o
institutions, great is our sin' – Charles Darwin, *Voyage of the Beagle*

PENGUIN BOOKS

HISTORY OF CIVILISATION

# THE AGE OF REVOLUTION

## EUROPE 1789-1848

E. J. Hobsbawm

# Space to Dream

Space
to Dream

# THE ATLAS OF
# Medieval Man

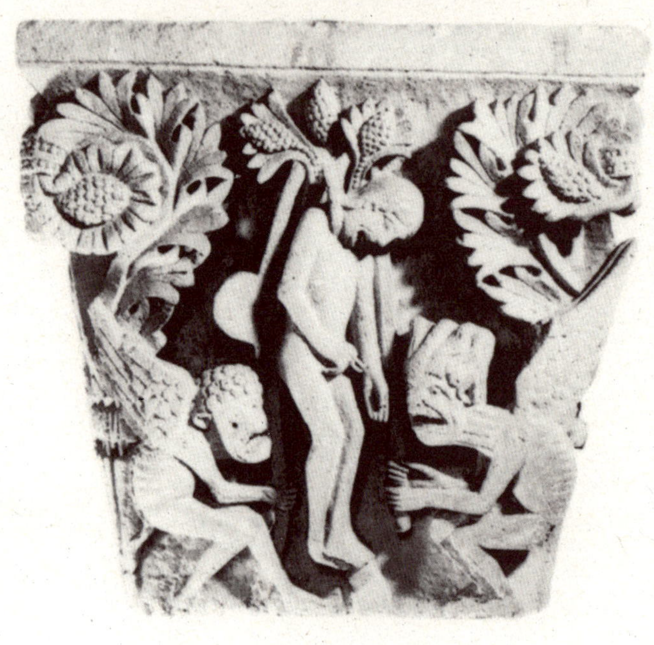

*Penguin Reference Books*

# THE PENGUIN ATLAS OF WORLD HISTORY

*Vol. 1: From the Beginning to the Eve of the French Revolution*

# Günter Grass

---

# My Century

*Translated by Michael Henry Heim*

# THE GENERATIONS OF MEN

*'The Generations of Men run on in the tide of Time,*
*But leave their destin'd lineaments permanent for ever and ever.'*

BLAKE: *Milton*

JORGE LUIS BORGES

# A UNIVERSAL HISTORY OF INFAMY

*Translated by Norman Thomas di Giovanni*

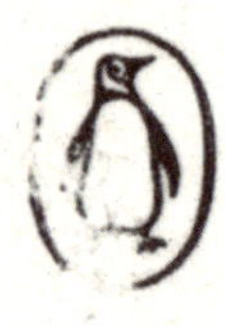

PENGUIN BOOKS

# ECONOMIC HISTORY OF EUROPE

A C T I V E   H I S T O R Y

# THE GROWTH OF WESTERN CIVILISATION

Don Scott & Lindsay Dann

NELSON

ACTIVE HISTORY

# THE GROWTH OF WESTERN CIVILISATION

Don Scott & Lindsay Dann

NELSON

GEORGE ORWELL

# *Nineteen Eighty-Four*

PENGUIN BOOKS

# NINETEEN EIGHTY-FOUR

A NOVEL

GEORGE ORWELL

Jorge Luis Borges

*with Margarita Guerrero*

# The Book of Imaginary Beings

*Revised* [illegible] *of a Strug*[illegible]
[illegible] by Schocken Books Inc.

Penguin Books

# THE NEW CAMBRIDGE MODERN HISTORY

ADVISORY COMMITTEE
G.N.CLARK J.R.M.BUTLER J.P.T.BURY
THE LATE E.A.BENIANS

VOLUME XII
(*second edition*)

# THE SHIFTING BALANCE OF WORLD FORCES
# 1898–1945

ALEXANDER SOLZHENITSYN

# *The First Circle*

Translated from the Russian
by Michael Guybon

COLLINS

# FIGURE ED EPISODII DEL-LA DIVINA COMMEDIA ⚜

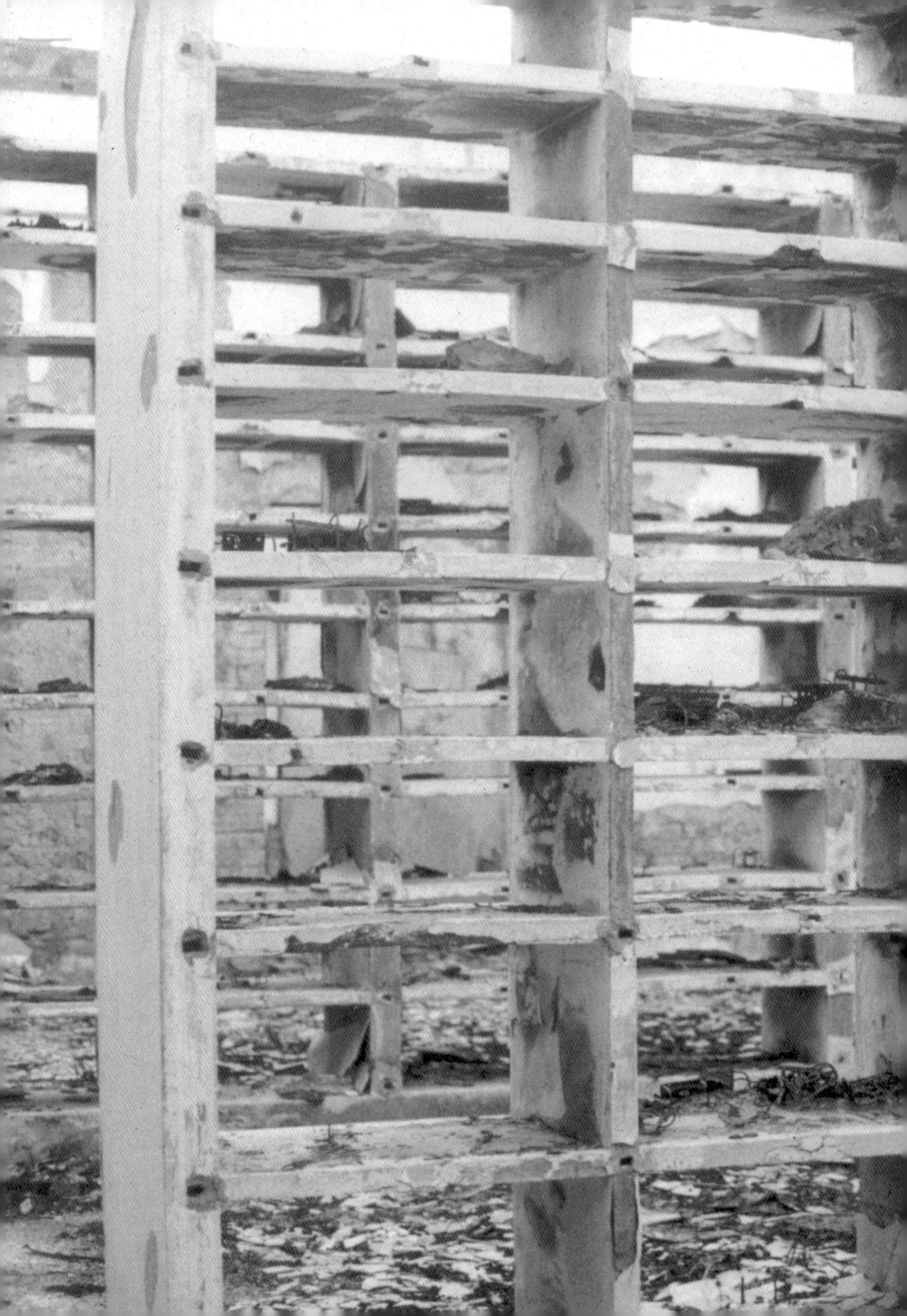

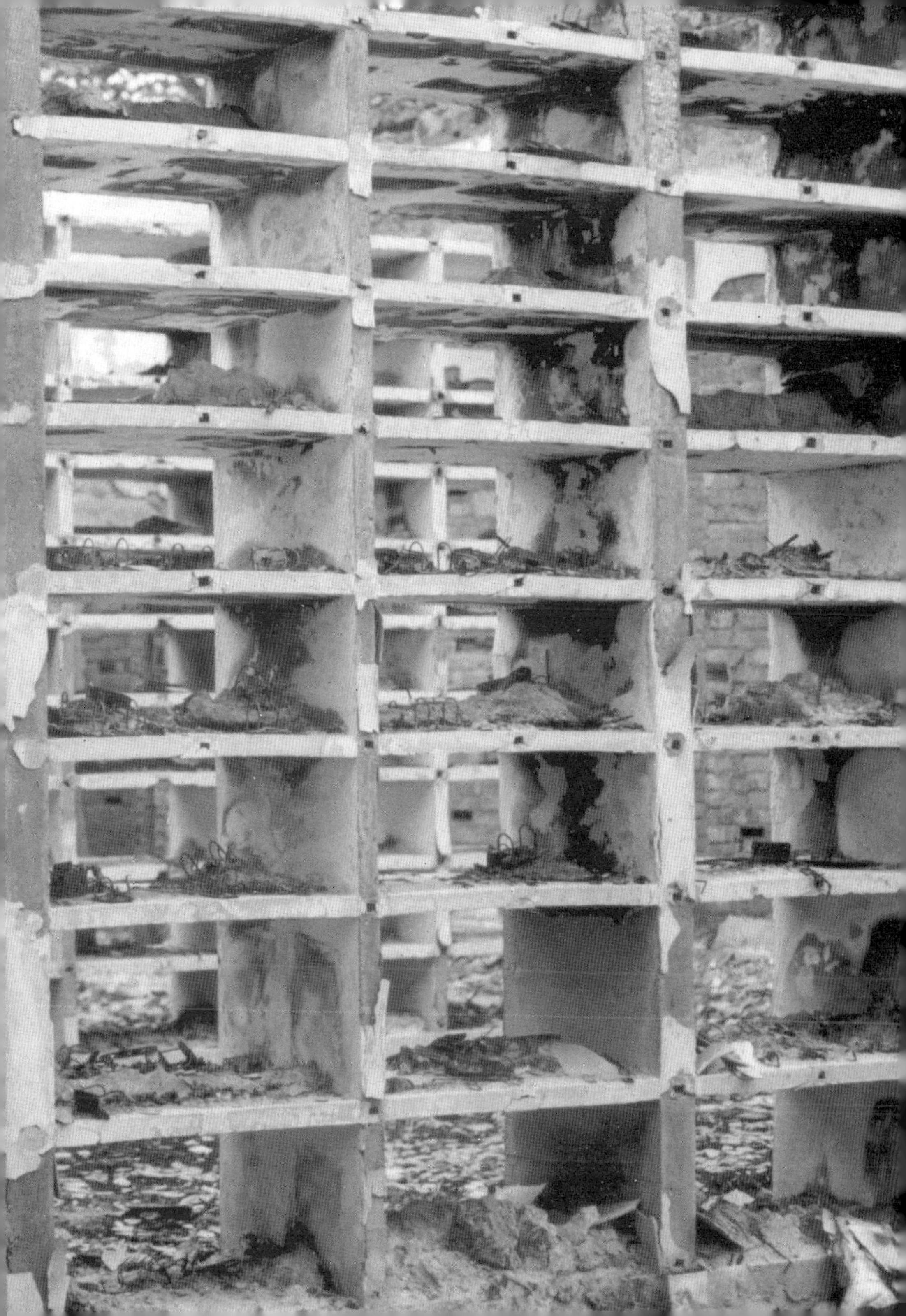

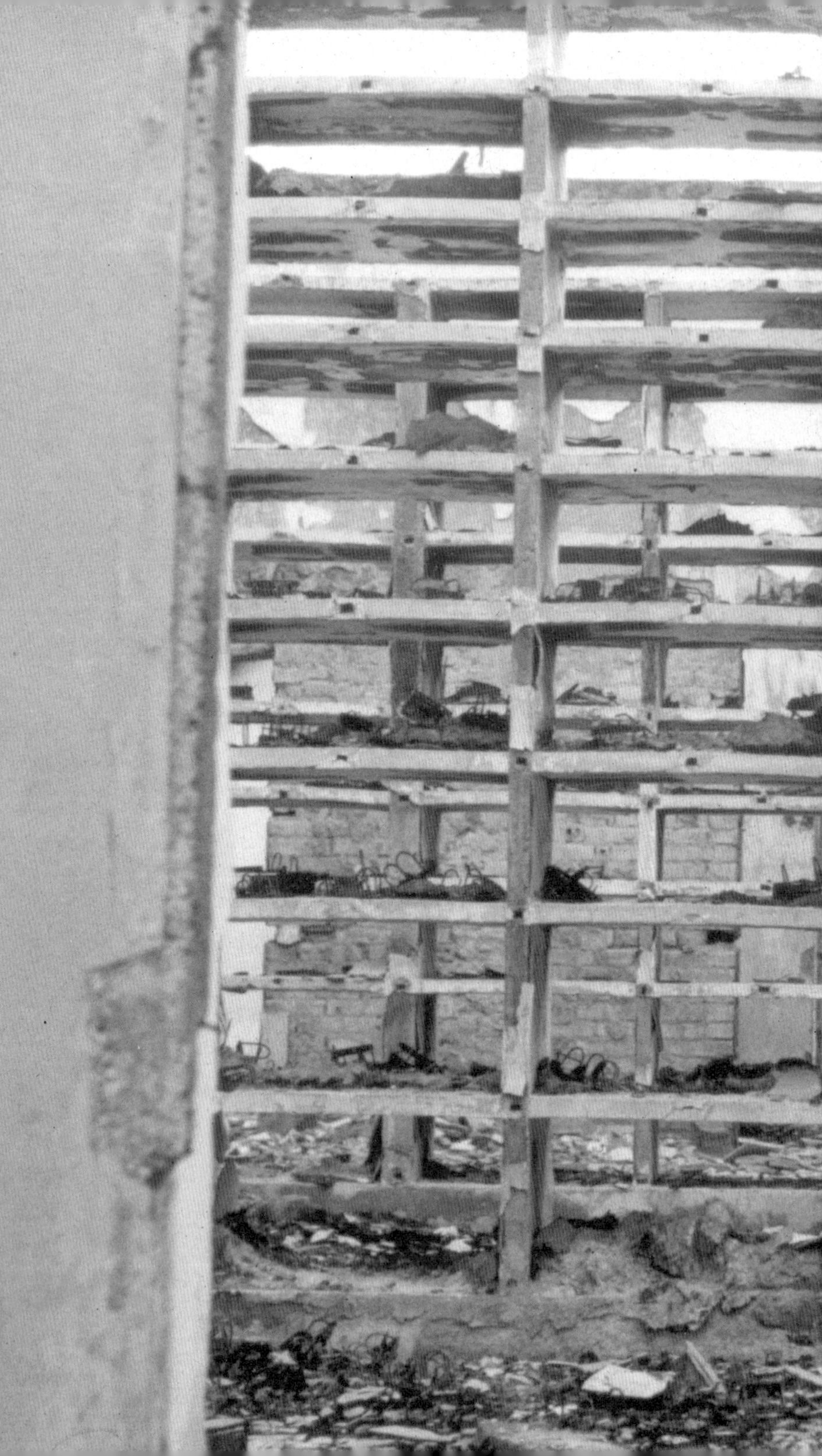

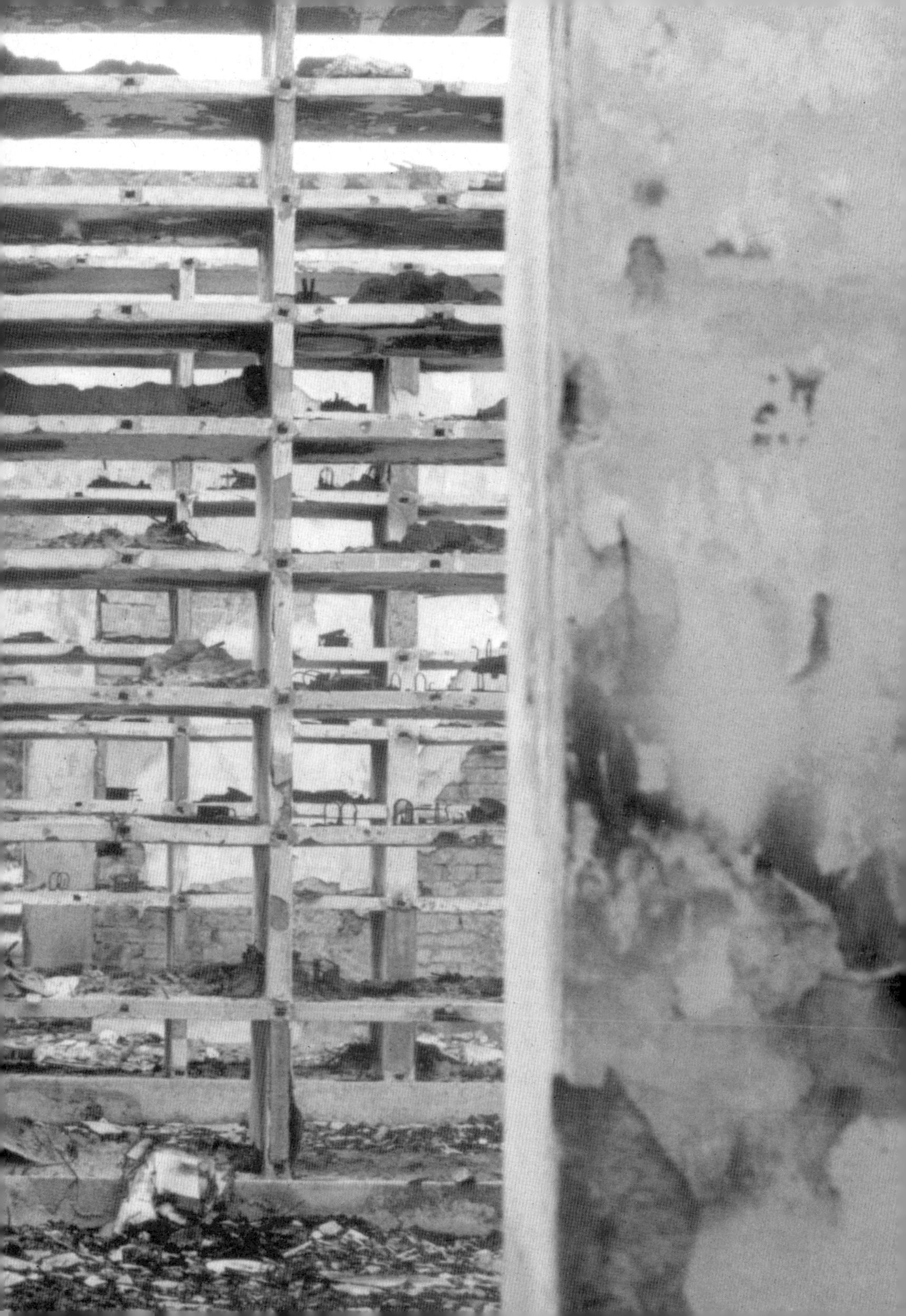

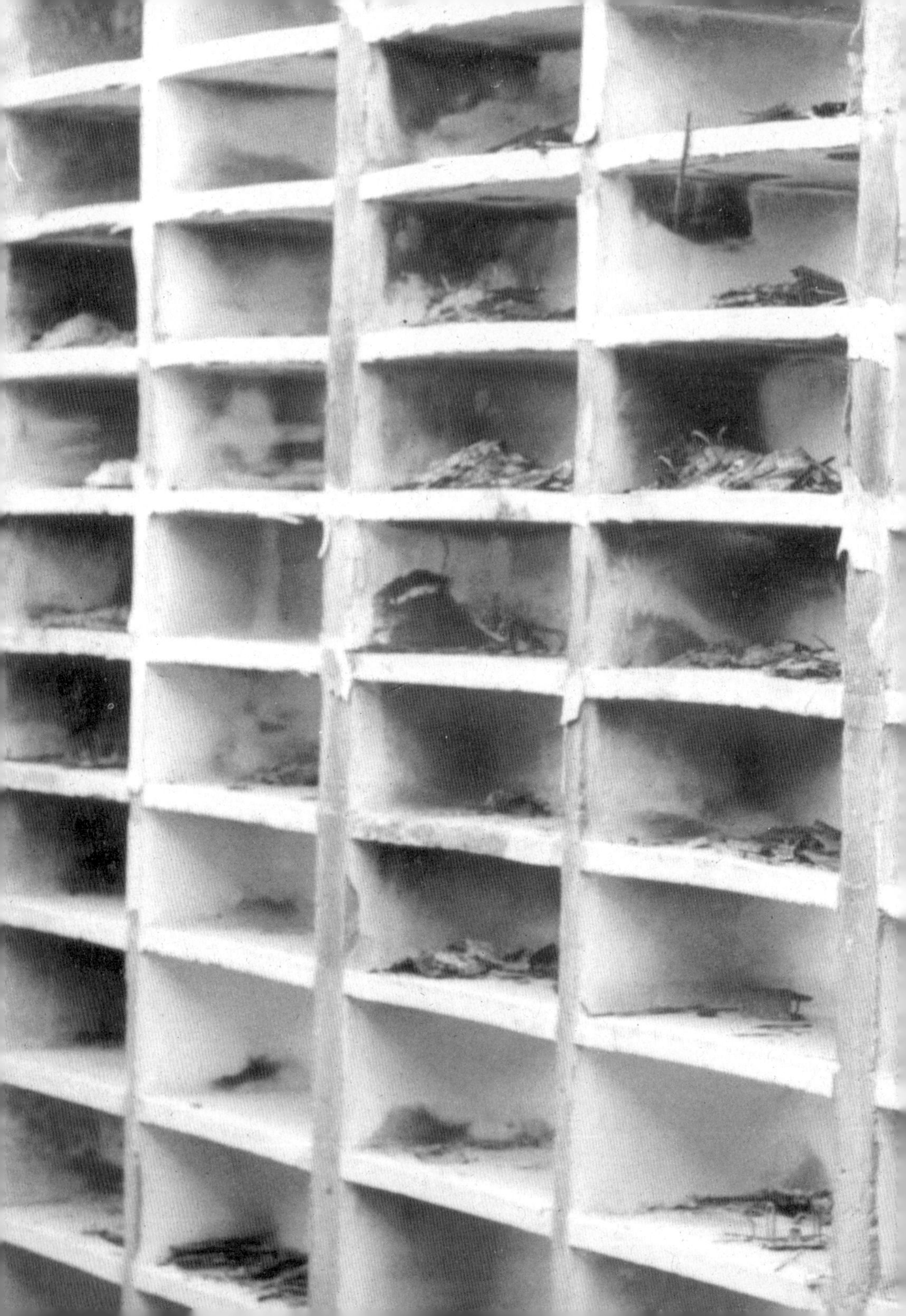

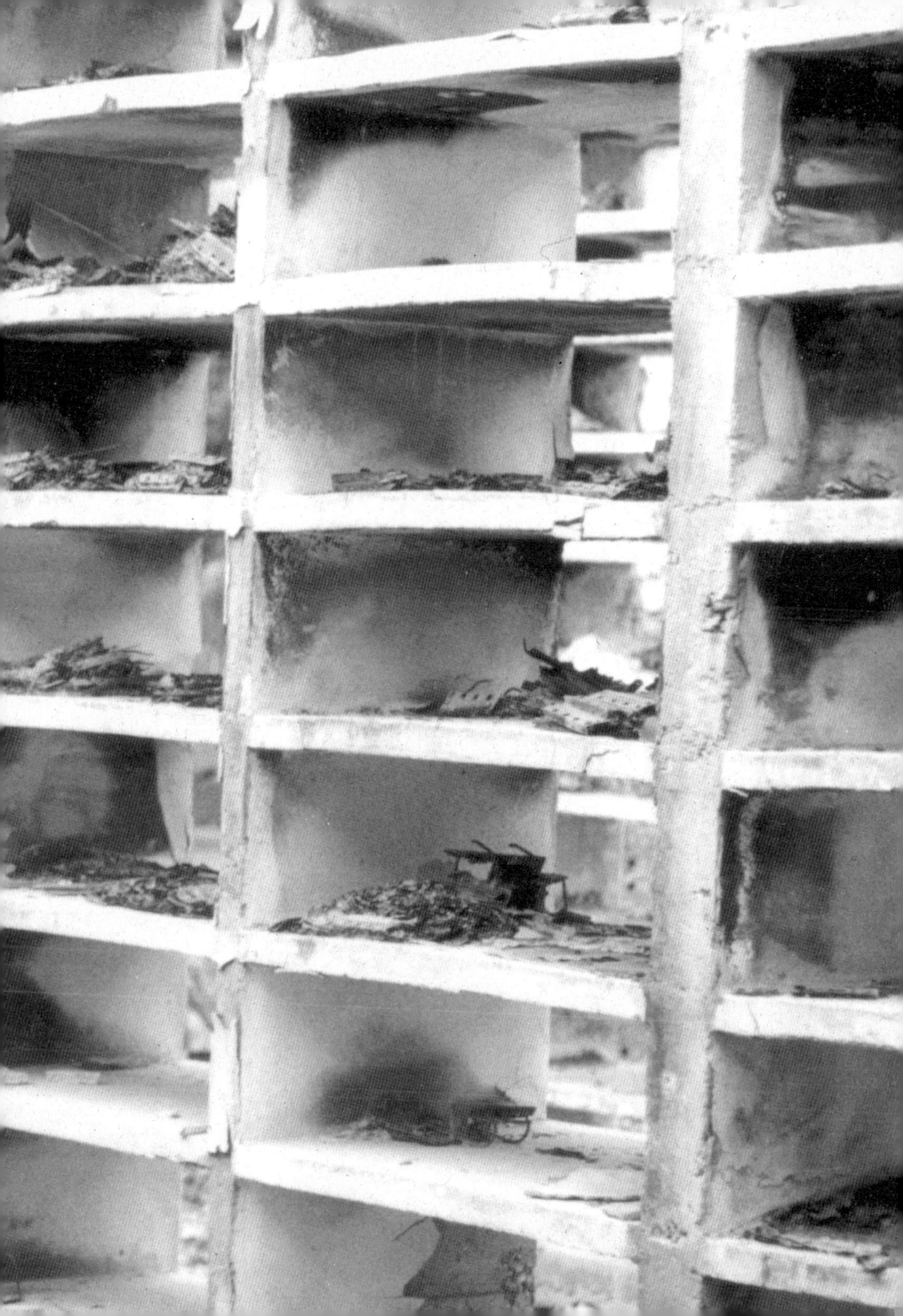

# THE
# CONCISE OXFORD
# DICTIONARY

OMPACT SCHOOL & OFFICE EDITION

# WEBSTER'S
# NEW WORLD
# DICTIONARY

David B. Guralnik, Editor in Chief

# Basic English Usage

Michael Swan

# Basic English Usage

Michael Swan

# THE CONCISE OXFORD DICTIONARY

## OF CURRENT ENGLISH

BASED ON
The Oxford English Dictionary
AND ITS SUPPLEMENTS

FIRST EDITED BY
H. W. Fowler and F. G. Fowler

SEVENTH EDITION

Edited by J. B. Sykes

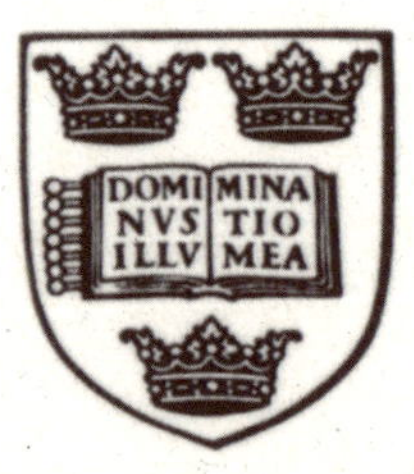


OXFORD

# THE OXFORD
# SCHOOL DICTIONARY

Dont look
over the this
nage

# ESSAY WRITING FOR STUDENTS

# Communication Skills in Practice

John Eastwood Ronald Mac

# A Basic English Grammar with Exercise

self-study editi

Oxford University P

# A Practical English Grammar

Writing Matters

# Writing Tasks

Writing Matters

# SCHINDLER'S ARK

**Thomas Keneally**

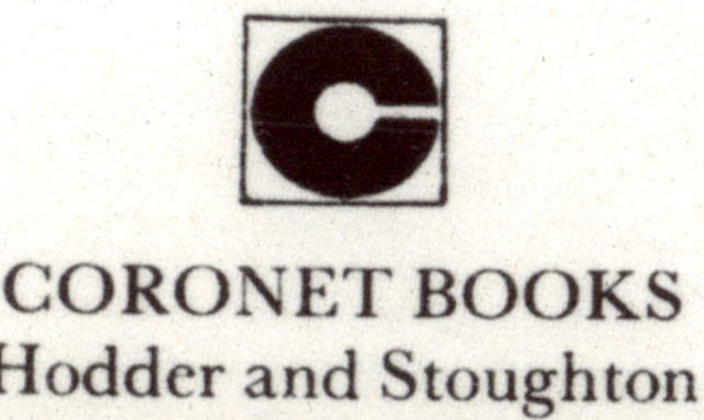

CORONET BOOKS
Hodder and Stoughton

# *Words*

JEAN-PAUL SARTRE

TRANSLATED BY
IRENE CLEPHANE

PENGUIN BOOKS

IN ASSOCIATION WITH
HAMISH HAMILTON

*Günter Grass*

# ON WRITING AND POLITICS

## *1967-1983*

*Translated by Ralph Manheim*

*Introduction by Salman Rushdie*

PENGUIN BOOKS

# LEARNING REMEMBERING AND KNOWING

# *Writing and Reading to Learn*

Portugal colonizou Timor-Leste em 1695. O Japão ocupou Timor-Leste em 1942–45 (foram mortas 40.000–70.000 pessoas). A Indonésia invadiu Timor-Leste em 1975, durante a ditadura militar de Suharto (1966–98). A resistência à ocupação indonésia permeou todos os aspectos da vida quotidiana. Foram mortos 200.000 timorenses (1 em cada 3) durante a ocupação (1975–99).[1] Também houve violência indirecta, na forma de fome / pobreza forçada / negação da independência económica.[2] No início dos anos 1990, Timor-Leste era a província mais pobre da Indonésia.[3] Os níveis de iliteracia eram o dobro dos verificados na segunda pior província.[4] Em 1996, a taxa de mortalidade infantil entre os timorenses situava-se entre as 5 piores do mundo.[5] As mulheres timorenses eram alvo de violência e abusos sistemáticos, associados a vergonha / silêncio;[6] programas de esterilização coerciva;[7] exclusão da educação (em 1994, 2 em cada 3 mulheres nunca tinham frequentado a escola).[8] Os países ocidentais patrocinavam o regime de Suharto. Os EUA apoiavam o anti-comunismo de Suharto.[9] A CIA forneceu às Forças Armadas indonésias listas de comunistas em 1965.[10] (500.000–1.000.000 comunistas indonésios / sindicalistas / feministas foram assassinados em 1965–66).[11] A Indonésia tornou-se um centro de investimento em produção industrial para as multinacionais do Ocidente (em 1983 era o segundo maior do mundo).[12] Ao longo dos anos 1980 e 1990, o RU forneceu à Indonésia aviões Hawk de ataque ao solo; os EUA venderam à Indonésia aviões Bronco / aviões Skyhawk / helicópteros Bell (todos eles utilizados para bombardear campos de refugiados em Timor-leste).[13] A Austrália foi a única nação a reconhecer de jure a soberania da Indonésia em Timor-Leste.[14] Tentou convencer (em vão) as Nações Unidas a seguir o seu exemplo. Desenvolveu uma forte ligação com as forças armadas indonésias (TNI) / assinou um acordo conjunto de segurança em 1995 / forneceu formação militar às forças indonésias nas décadas de 1980 e 1990.[15] A 30 de Agosto de 1999, 98% dos timorenses participaram num acto eleitoral patrocinado pelas Nações Unidas (desafiando a violência sistemática das TNI / milícias); 78% votaram a favor da independência.[16] Na sequência do anúncio do resultado da votação as TNI / milícias mataram vários milhares de civis (desconhece-se o número exacto); 200.000 timorenses foram levados à força para Timor Ocidental / outras regiões da Indonésia;[17] as mulheres timorenses foram alvo de abusos sexuais sistemáticos por parte da Indonésia;[18] 60–80% dos edifícios existentes foram destruídos;[19] depois da INTERFET (força de manutenção da paz liderada pela Austrália) e da UNTAET ( administração transitória das Nações Unidas ), Timor-Leste foi reconhecido como país independente em 20 de Maio de 2002.

1965年、ポルトガルが東ティモールを植民地化。1942–45年、東ティモールは日本軍によって占領された(40,000–70,000人もの命が奪われた)。1975年、スハルト独裁政権(1966–98年)の最中、インドネシア軍が東ティモールに侵入。インドネシア軍の占領に対する反抗心は、全ての生ける者の心に刻み込まれた。インドネシアの制圧下(1975–99年)、およそ200,000人もの東ティモール人の命が奪われた(3人に1人の割合)。[1] その暴力は、直接的なものだけではなく、飢餓/強いられた貧困/閉ざされた経済的独立への道など、間接的なものでもあった。[2] 1990年代初頭までに、東ティモールはインドネシアで最も貧しい州となった。[3] 識字率の低さは、東ティモールに次ぐ州よりも、更に2倍劣るものであった。[4] 1996年、東ティモールにおける幼児の死亡率は、全世界でも最も高いといわれる5ヶ国の中に名前をあげられるに至った。[5] 最も顕著な暴力は、東ティモールの女性に向けられた、羞恥心ゆえの沈黙につけこんだ組織的な強姦、[6] 不妊手術の強制プログラム、[7] 教育からの除外(1994年、3人に2人の女性は学校に通ったことがない)というものであった。[8] 西欧諸国は、スハルト政権の後援にまわった。米国は、スハルトの反共産主義に対して、寛容な目を向けた。[9] 1965年、CIAはインドネシア軍に、共産主義者のリストを提供。[10] (1965–66年、およそ500,000–1,000,000人ものインドネシア共産主義者、労働組合活動員、女性解放論者が殺害された。)[11] インドネシアは、西欧各国の製造業に携わる多国籍企業からの、投資先の中心となった(1983年までには、全世界で2位)。[12] 1980—90年代にかけて、英国はホーク地上攻撃機を、そして、米国はブロンコ戦闘機、スカイホーク戦闘機、ベル・戦闘ヘリコプターを販売した(これらの戦闘機は、東ティモールの難民キャンプを爆撃するために使用された)。[13] オーストラリアは、東ティモールを道理上の独立国家として認める、唯一の国家であった。[14] またオーストラリアは、国連にも認められるよう運動を起こした(失敗に終わる)。また、これがきっかけでインドネシア国民軍(TNI)との密接な関係を築き上げ、1995年、安全保障条約を締結し、1980—90年代にかけて、インドネシア軍に対して、軍事訓練を提供した。[15] 1999年8月30日、国連の援助の下に実施された投票(TNIやその軍隊に挑む目的)には、98%もの東ティモール人が参加し、その78%が独立を求める結果となった。[16] その投票結果の発表後、TNIとその軍隊は、数千人におよぶ市民(正確な数字は不明)を殺害し、200,000人もの東ティモール人が西ティモールやインドネシアのその他の地域に強制移送され、[17] 東ティモールの女性は組織的な性的虐待を強いられ、[18] 60–80%の建物は破壊された。[19] INTERFET(オーストラリアを主体とする多国籍平和維持軍)の派遣、UNTAET(国連東ティモール暫定統治機構)発足の後、2002年5月20日に東ティモールは独立国家として認められた。

Portugál komesa koloniza Timor iha tinan 1695. Japaun okupa tiha Timor-Leste iha tinan 1942 to'o 1945 (ema entre na'in 40,000 to'o 70,000 maka mate). Indonézia invade Timor-Leste iha tinan 1975, durante ditadura militár Suharto nian (1966–1998). Rezisténsia kontra okupasaun Indonézia mosu iha ema hotuhotu nia moris (1975–99). Timor-oan na'in 200,000 maka mate durante Indonézia nia okupasaun (1975–1999).[1] Indiretamente, violénsia mós mosu liu hosi hamlaha, forsa ema nia moris sai kiak no mós nega ema nia independénsia ekonómika.[2] Komesa tinan 1999, Timor-Leste maka provínsia ida kiak liu iha Indonézia.[3] Nivel analfabetizmu nian aas liu fali dala rua kompara ho nivel provínsia seluk ne'ebé Timor-Leste tuir iha Indonézia.[4] Iha 1996, Timor-Leste nia taxa mortalidade foin-moris nian hamutuk ho país lima aas liu iha mundu.[5] Violénsia-boot maka hamosu kontra Timor-feto sira liu hosi violasaun sistemátika asosiada ho dezónra (moe) / siléensiu ne'ebé mosu;[6] programa esterilizasaun koersiva;[7] eskluzaun hosi edukasaun (iha 1994, feto 2 hosi 3 nunka bá eskola).[8] País osidentál sira maka esponsor rejime Suharto nian. EUA (Amérika) fó laran ba Suharto nia rejime anti-komunista ne'e.[9] CIA maka prepara lista ema komunista / sindikatu sira / feminista sira nia naran ba militár Indonézia nian iha tinan 1965.[10] (Indonézia nia komunista sira / sindikatu sira / feminista na'in 500,000–1,000,000 maka ema oho iha tinan 1965–66.)[11] Indonézia sai hanesan sentru ba investimentu iha fábriku ba kompanhia multinasionál país Osidentál nian (iha 1983 segundu iha mundu).[12] Iha tinan 1980 to'o 1990, Reino Unido fa'an aviaun-funu Hawk ba Indonézia; Estados Unidos fa'an aviaun-funu Bronco / Skyhawk / Bell Helicopter (aviaun sira uza hodi bomba kampu refujiadu sira iha Timor-Leste laran).[13] Austrália maka úniku país iha mundu ne'ebé rekonhese de jure Indonézia nia soberania iha Timor-Leste.[14] Austrália halo lobby ba Nações Unidas (laiha susesu) atu halo tuir nia. Austrália dezenvolve relasaun di'ak ho militár Indonézia nian (TNI) / asina akordu kona ba seguransa iha 1995 / fornese treinu militár ba forsa Indonézia iha dékada 1980 ho 1990.[15] Iha 30 de Agostu tinan 1999, Timor-oan 98% maka vota referendu ne'ebé ONU halo (hasoru violénsia sistemátika hosi TNI / milísia); 78% maka vota ba independénsia.[16] Hafoin anunsia tiha rezultadu referendu nian, TNI ho milísia oho tiha ema sivíl rihun balu (númeru loloos ema lahatene); Timor-oan naín 200,000 maka sira obriga bá hotu Timor Indonézia / ho parte Indonézia nian sira seluk;[17] Timor-feto sira sofre abuzu seksuál sistemátika;[18] uma 60–80% maka sira estraga hotu.[19] Hafoin INTERFET (forsa komanda hosi Austrália), UNTAET (autoridade tranzitória UN nian) liu tiha, Timor-Leste hetan rekonhesimentu hanesan país independente iha dia 20 de Maiu tinan 2002.

Portugal mulai menjajahi Timor-Leste pada tahun 1695. Di tahun 1942–45, Jepang menduduki Timor-Leste (40,000–70,000 orang tewas). Indonesia menyerbu Timor-Leste di tahun 1975 di bawah diktatur militer Suharto (1966–98). Perlawanan terhadap pendudukan Indonesia menembus seluruh segi kehidupan. Sebanyak 200,000 penduduk Timor-Leste tewas akibat pendudukan itu (1975–99).[1] Ada pun kekerasan yang tidak langsung melalui kelaparan / kemiskinan terpaksa / peniadaan kebebasan ekonomi.[2] Pada awal 1990an, Timor-Leste adalah propinsi Indonesia yang paling miskin.[3] Tingkat kebutahurufan 2 kali lebih dibanding dengan tingkat kebuatahurufan yang paling buruk para propinsi berikutnya.[4] Di 1996, angka kematian bayi di Timor-Leste termasuk ke 5 paling buruk.[5] Kekerasan besar-besaran dilakukan terhadap wanita Timor-Leste melalui pemerkosaan sistematis, dengan perasaan malu / diam yang berhubungan;[6] program-program pemandulan paksa;[7] peniadaan dari pendidikan (di 1994, 2 dari 3 wanita tidak pernah masuk sekolah).[8] Negara-negara barat mendukung rezim Suharto. Amerika Serikat bersimpatisan dengan antikomunisnya Suharto.[9] Di tahun 1965 CIA menyediakan militer Indonesia dengan daftar nama-nama para pengikut komunisme.[10] (500,000–1,000,000 pengikut komunisme / aktivis kaum buruh / aktivis feminis Indonesia dibunuh di tahun 1965–66).[11] Indonesia menjadi pusat untuk investasi pabrik oleh para multinasional barat (sampai 1983, terbesar ke dua di dunia).[12] Di tahun 1980an dan 1990an, Inggris menjual pesawat serang darat Hawk kepada Indonesia; AS menjual pesawat Bronco / Skyhawk / helikopter Bell (semuanya digunakan untuk membom kampung-kampung pengungsi di Timor-Leste).[13] Australia adalah satu-satunya negara yang mengakui kedaulatan de jure Indonesia atas Timor-Leste.[14] Ia melobi PBB (tiada sukses) untuk mengikutinya. Ia memperkembangkan persahabatan erat dengan militer Indonesia (TNI) / menandatangani pakta keamanan bersama di 1995 / menyediakan latihan militer untuk angkatan-angkatan Indonesia sepanjang tahun 1980an dan 1990an.[15] Pada 30 Agustus 1999, 98% orang Timor-Leste turut mengikuti pemungutan suara yang disponsori oleh PBB (menentangi kekerasan sistematis dari TNI / milisi); 78% memilih kemerdekaan.[16] Setelah pengumuman hasil suara tersebut TNI dan milisinya membunuh beberapa ribu masyarakat sipil (angka yang benar tidak diketahui); 200,000 orang Timor-Leste dipaksa pergi ke Timor Barat / daerah-daerah lain di Indonesia;[17] perempuan Timor Timur mengalami kekerasan seksual sistematis;[18] 60%–80% dari semua bangunan dimusnahkan.[19] Setelah INTERFET (pasukan perdamaian yang dipimpin oleh Australia) dan UNTAET, Timor-Leste diakui sebagai negara yang merdeka pada tanggal 20 Mei 2002.

Portugal colonised East Timor in 1695. Japan occupied East Timor 1942–45 (40,000–70,000 were killed). Indonesia invaded East Timor in 1975, during Suharto's military dictatorship (1966–98). Resistance to Indonesian occupation permeated all facets of life. 200,000 East Timorese (1 in 3 people) were killed during the occupation (1975–99).[1] Violence was also indirect, through starvation / enforced poverty / the denial of economic independence.[2] By the early 1990s, East Timor was the poorest province of Indonesia.[3] Illiteracy levels were two times the levels of the next worst province.[4] In 1996, the East Timorese infant mortality rate was amongst the worst five on earth.[5] Significant violence was directed at East Timorese women, through systematic rape, with the associated shame / silence;[6] coercive sterilisation programmes;[7] exclusion from education (in 1994, two in three women had never attended school).[8] Western countries sponsored Suharto's regime. The USA looked kindly on Suharto's anti-communism.[9] The CIA provided the Indonesian military with lists of communists in 1965.[10] (500,000–1,000,000 Indonesian communists / trade union activists / feminists were murdered 1965–66).[11] Indonesia became a centre for investment in manufacturing by Western multinationals (by 1983 the second largest on earth).[12] Through 1980s–90s, the UK sold Indonesia Hawk ground-attack aircraft; the US sold Indonesia Bronco aircraft / Skyhawk aircraft / Bell helicopters (all used to bomb refugee camps within East Timor).[13] Australia was the only nation to recognise de jure Indonesian sovereignty over East Timor.[14] It lobbied the United Nations (not successfully) to follow suit. It developed close ties with the Indonesian military (TNI) / signed a joint security agreement in 1995 / supplied military training to Indonesian forces through 1980s–90s.[15] 30 August 1999, 98% of East Timorese voted in a UN-sponsored ballot (defying systematic violence by TNI / their militia); 78% for independence.[16] Following the ballot result announcement the TNI / their militia killed several thousand civillians (exact number unknown); 200,000 East Timorese were forcibly removed to West Timor / other parts of Indonesia;[17] East Timorese women suffered systematic sexual assault;[18] 60–80% of all buildings were destroyed.[19] After INTERFET (Australian-led peacekeeping force), UNTAET (UN-sponsored transitional authority), East Timor was recognised as an independent nation on 20 May 2002.

[1] G. Aditjondro, *In the Shadow of Mt Ramelau: The Impact of the Occupation of East Timor*, Indonesian Documentation and Information Centre, Leiden, 1994, p 9. [2] Miranda Sissons, *From One Day to Another: Violations of Women's Reproductive and Sexual Rights in East Timor*, Melbourne, p 8. [3] G.W. Jones and Y. Raharjo, *People, Land and Sea, Development Challenges in Eastern Indonesia*, Canberra, 1995; Ministry of Health, Republic of Indonesia, *Indonesia Health Profile 1994*, Attachments, Ministry of Health Centre for Data, Jakarta, 1994, II.B.1–II.B.7. [4] Central Bureau of Statistics (Indonesia) and State Ministry of Population / National Family Planning Co-ordinating Board and Ministry of Health and Macro International Inc., *Indonesia: Health and Demographic Survey, 1994*, Calverton Maryland, 1995, pp 14–19; also, *Indonesia Health Profile 1994*, Attachments, II.B.2, II.B.4, p 34. [5] United Nations Department for Economic and Social Information and Policy Analysis, *World Population Report 1996*, New York, 1996. [6] Sissons, p 9. [7] Sissons, pp 11–33. [8] *Indonesia: Health and Demographic Survey, 1994*, Table 2.5.4, p 18. [9] Philip Liechte, CIA officer in Jakarta, as quoted by John Pilger, *Hidden Agendas*, London, 1998, p 285; Mark Aarons and Robert Down, *East Timor: A Western Made Tragedy*, Sydney, 1992, p 26; Robert Cribb, "Introduction", in Robert Cribb (ed.), *The Indonesian Killings 1965–1966: Studies from Java and Bali*, Clayton, 1990, p 5. [10] Ralph W. McGehee, *Deadly Deceits: My 25 Years in the CIA*, New York, 1983, pp 57–8; Gabriel Kolko, *Confronting the Third World: US Foreign Policy 1945–1980*, New York, 1989, pp 173–183; David Ransome, "The Berkeley Mafia and the Indonesian Massacre", *Ramparts 9*, no. 4, October 1970, pp 27–29; Kathy Kadane, "Ex-agents Say CIA Compiled Death Lists for Indonesians", *San Francisco Examiner*, 20 May 1990, pp 1, 22. [11] KOPKAMTIB (Operational Command for the Restoration of Security and Order) (Official Indonesian Government) Survey 1966 (unpublished); quoted in Frank Palmos, "One Million Dead", *The Economist*, 20 August 1966, pp 727–728; Bruce Cleland, "Greatest Bloodbath in Indonesia's History" *Dawn 2*, August 1966; see also table summarising different estimates of Indonesians killed 1965–66, in Robert Cribb (ed.), *The Indonesian Killings 1965–1966: Studies from Java and Bali*, Clayton, 1990, p 12; including: *Repression and Exploitation in Indonesia*, Nottingham, 1974, p 9; Malcolm Caldwell and Ernst Utrecht, *Indonesia: An Alternative History*, Sydney, 1979; Benedict Nelson, "Afterword", *Indonesia 40*, 1985, p 53; Nawaz B. Mody, *Indonesia Under Suharto*, New Delhi, 1987, p 46. Some estimates of numbers killed between 1965–66 are as high as 2,000,000 people: see Bridget Mellor, "Political Killings in Indonesia", *New Statesman*, 5 August 1966, p 189. Hundreds of thousands were murdered in the subsequent thirty years. In 1983 alone, 200,000–300,000 were murdered in a crack-down in Java and Bali. More than 1,500,000 were imprisoned in political detention camps in the years immediately after the 1966 coup (Robert Cribb and Colin Brown, *Modern Indonesia: A History Since 1945*, London, 1995, p 130, 121). [12] The concentration of investment by Western multinational manufacturers was based largely on the favourable terms of Suharto's Foreign Investment Law 1967, and the violent suppression of organised labour throughout Indonesia. See Ernst Utrecht, "Indonesia's Foreign Private Corporate System, Past and Present", in Christine Doran (ed.), *Indonesian Politics: A Reader*, Townsville, 1987, pp 173–204. [13] Britain also sold Indonesia Sea Wolf and Rapier surface-to-air missiles, Tribal class frigates, Saracen armoured vehicles, and Tactica riot control vehicles. Indonesian special forces, Kopassus, were armed with Heckler and Koch automatic weapons from British Aerospace. These purchases were guaranteed through the UK Export Credit Guarantee Department. In 1998, the UK earned USD36 billion in arms exports (Pilger, pp 119–23). [14] James Gunn, *Timor: A People Betrayed*, Sydney, 1996, pp 345–9. [15] Gunn, pp 345–9. [16] United Nations Office of the High Commissioner for Human Rights, *Report of the International Commission of Inquiry on East Timor to the Secretary-General*, January 2000. [17] United Nations, *Report of the International Commission of Inquiry on East Timor*. [18] United Nations, *Report of the International Commission of Inquiry on East Timor*. [19] United Nations, *Report of the International Commission of Inquiry on East Timor*.

# FRANZ KAFKA

# THE CASTLE

*

*Translated from the German by*

WILLA AND EDWIN MUIR

*with additional material translated by*

EITHNE WILKINS AND
ERNST KAISER

PENGUIN BOOKS

# FRANZ KAFKA

# THE TRIAL

*Translated by* IDRIS PARRY

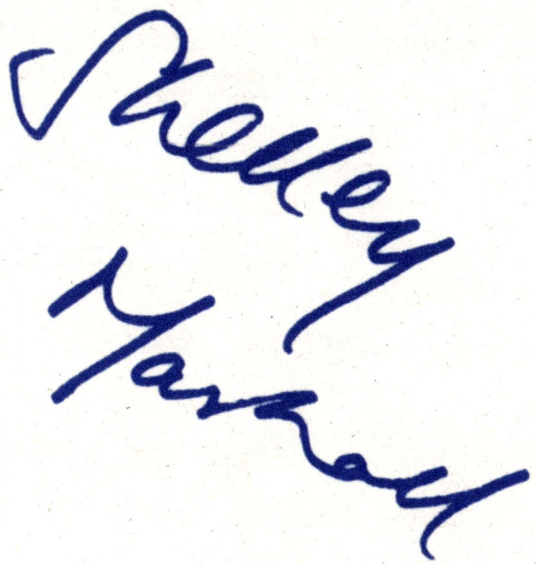

PENGUIN BOOKS

# THE GETTING OF WISDOM

# Descartes

## PHILOSOPHICAL WRITINGS

*A selection translated
and edited by*
Elizabeth Anscombe
and Peter Thomas Geach
*With an Introduction by*
Alexandre Koyré

Nelson's University Paperbacks
The Open University

# The Bell Jar

Look at mirror images
p. 105

FRANZ KAFKA

# Metamorphosis

## *AND OTHER STORIES*

TRANSLATED BY
WILLA AND EDWIN MUIR

# Parables for the Theatre

## Two Plays by Bertolt Brecht

---

## The Good Woman of Setzuan

## The Caucasian Chalk Circle

---

Revised English Versions
by Eric Bentley

# The Tragedy of
# KING LEAR

Edited by Russell Fraser

*The Signet Classic Shakespeare*
GENERAL EDITOR: SYLVAN BARNET
Revised and Updated Bibliography

A SIGNET CLASSIC
NEW AMERICAN LIBRARY

NEW YORK AND SCARBOROUGH, ONTARIO

*William Shakespeare*

# The Tragedy of *HAMLET* Prince of Denmark

Edited by Edward Hubler

*The Signet Classic Shakespeare*
GENERAL EDITOR: SYLVAN BARNET
Revised and Updated Bibliography

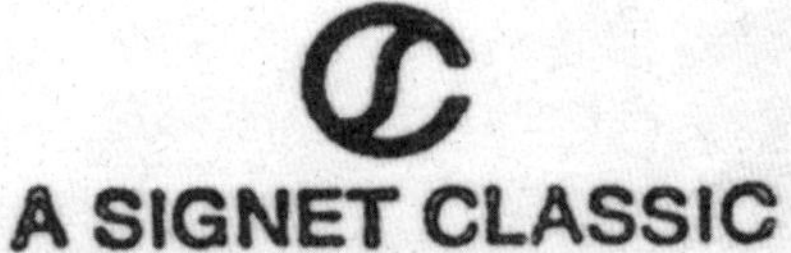

A SIGNET CLASSIC
NEW AMERICAN LIBRARY
NEW YORK AND SCARBOROUGH, ONTARIO

Italo Calvino

# MARCOVALDO

or

The seasons in the city

Translated from the Italian by William Weaver

THE WORLD'S CLASSICS

ARISTOTLE

# The Politics

*Translated by*

ERNEST BARKER

*Revised with an Introduction and Notes by*

R. F. STALLEY

# THE REPUBLIC OF PLATO

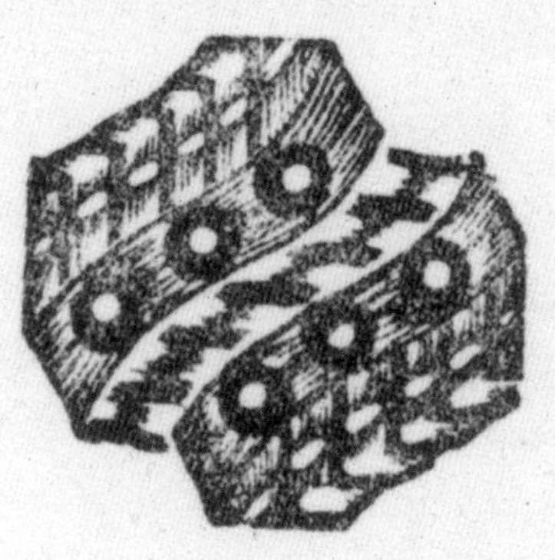

LEWIS CARROLL

# Alice's Adventures in Wonderland

Illustrations by

JOHN TENNIEL

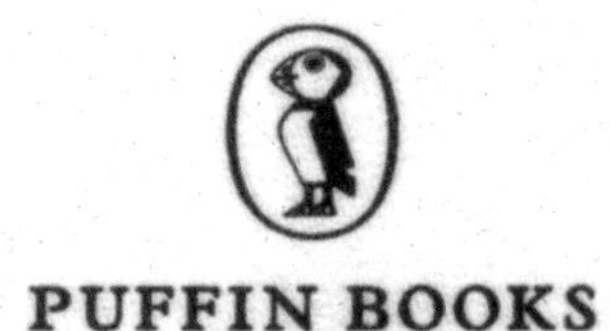

PUFFIN BOOKS

J.G. BALLARD

# *Hello America*

# *Waiting for Godot*

# SIX CHARACTERS IN SEARCH OF AN AUTHOR

*by*

LUIGI PIRANDELLO

*Translated by*

FREDERICK MAY

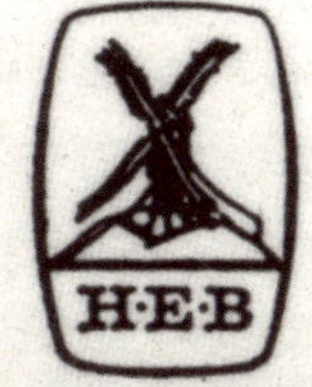

GOETHE

---

# FAUST

## PART ONE

TRANSLATED BY PHILIP WAYNE

—

PENGUIN BOOKS

# THE PLAGUE

ALBERT CAMUS

—

TRANSLATED FROM THE FRENCH BY
STUART GILBERT

—

It is as reasonable to represent one kind of imprisonment by another, as it is to represent anything that really exists by that which exists not! –

*'Robinson Crusoe's Preface' to the third volume of* Robinson Crusoe

DANIEL DEFOE

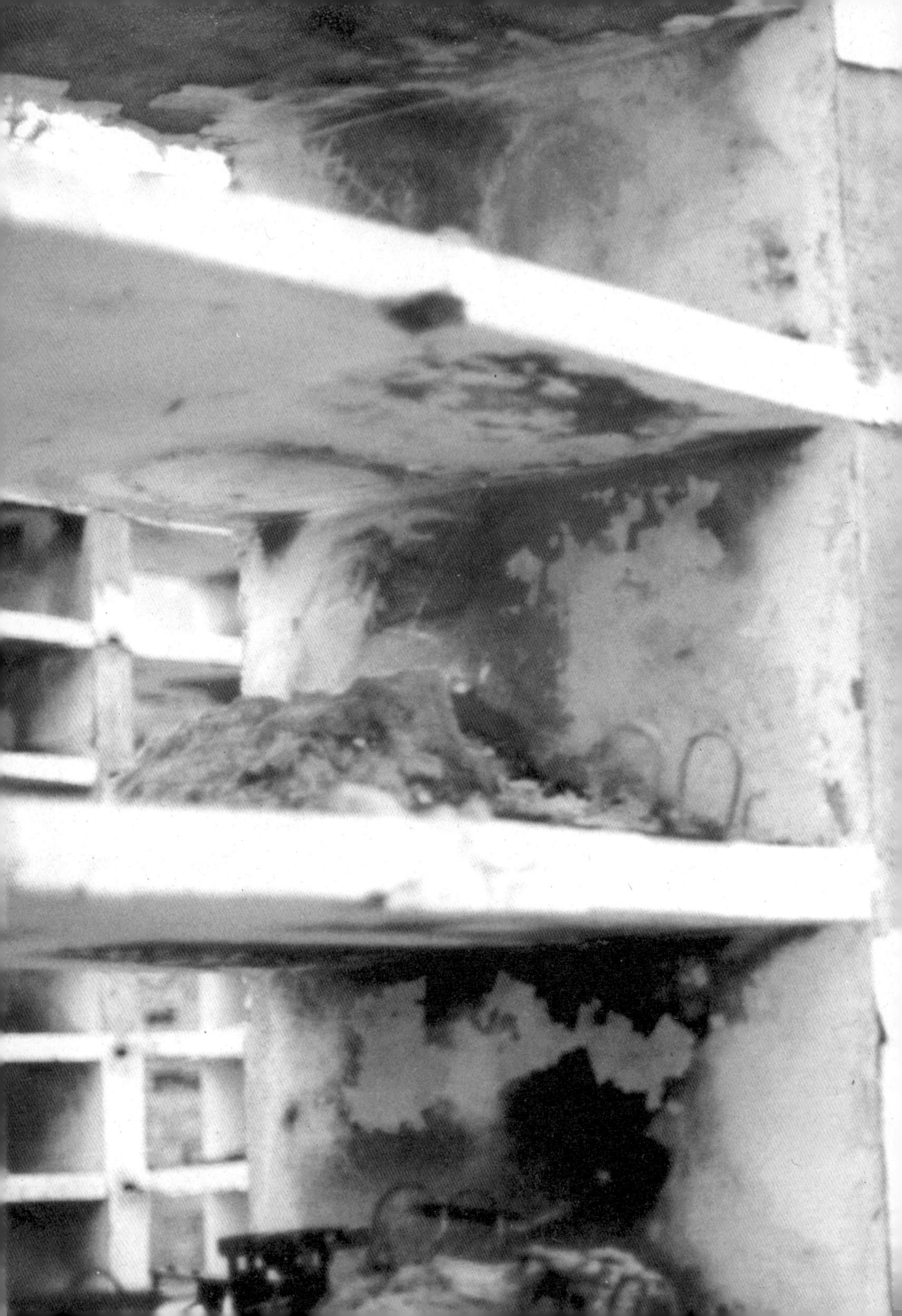

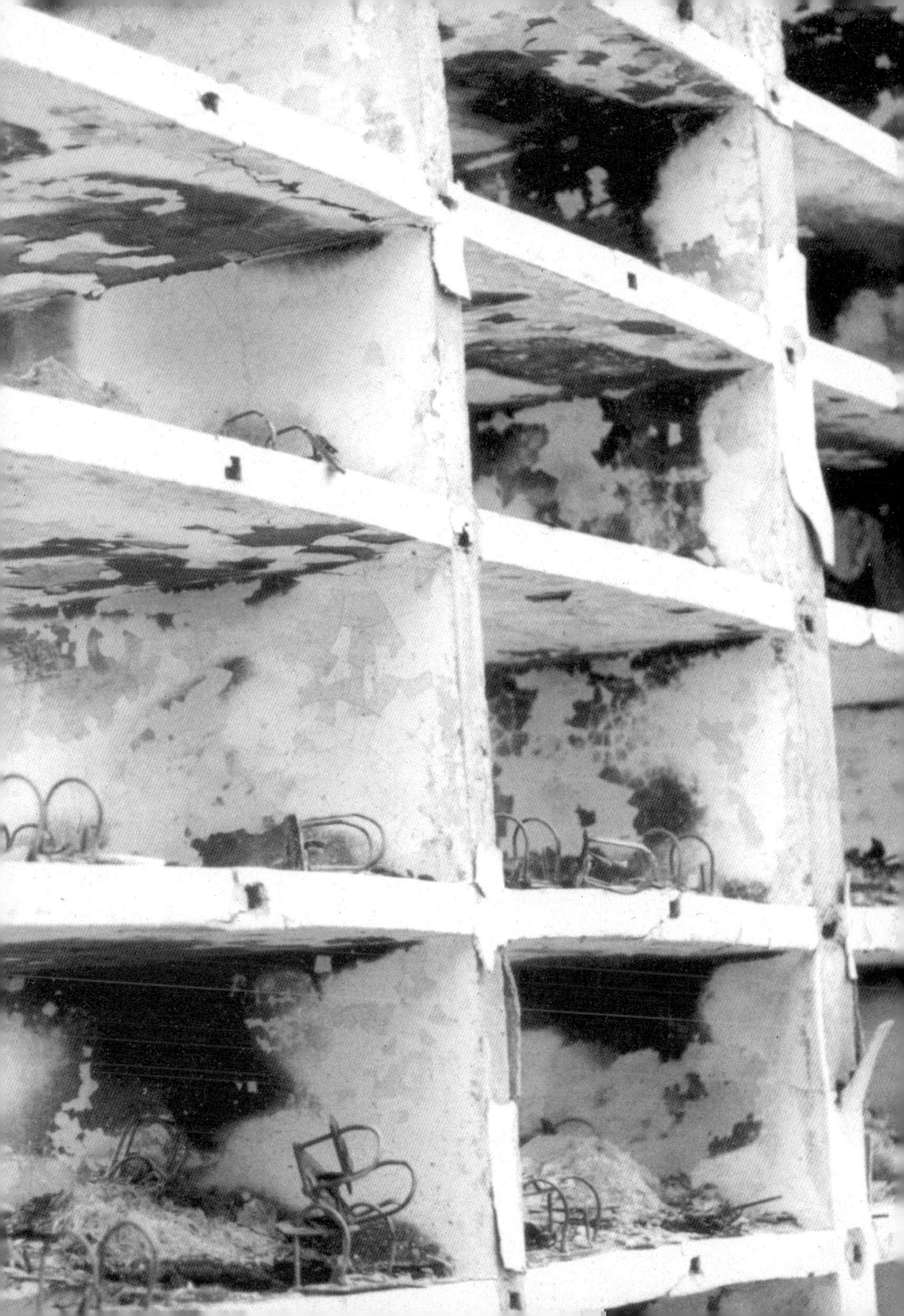

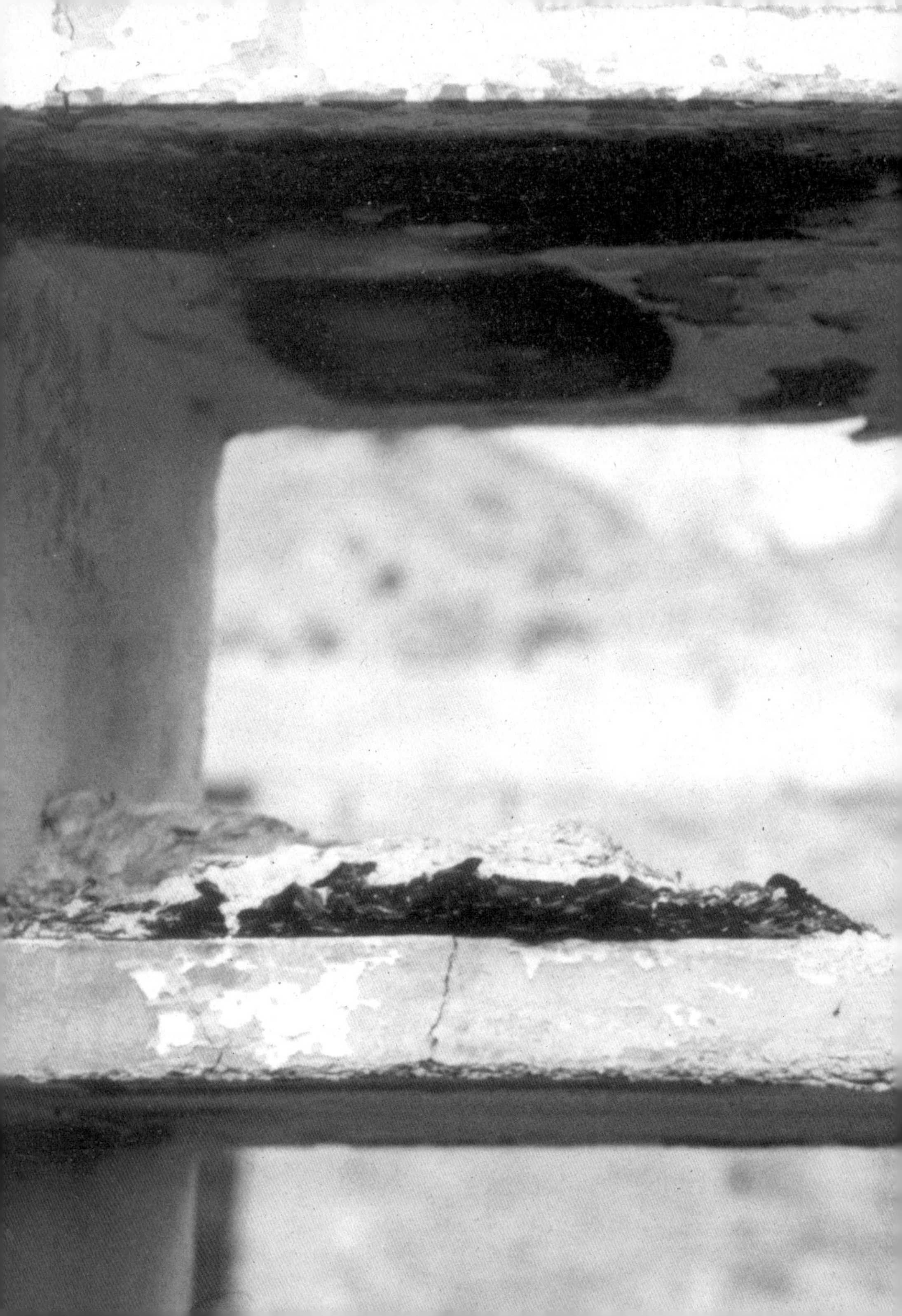

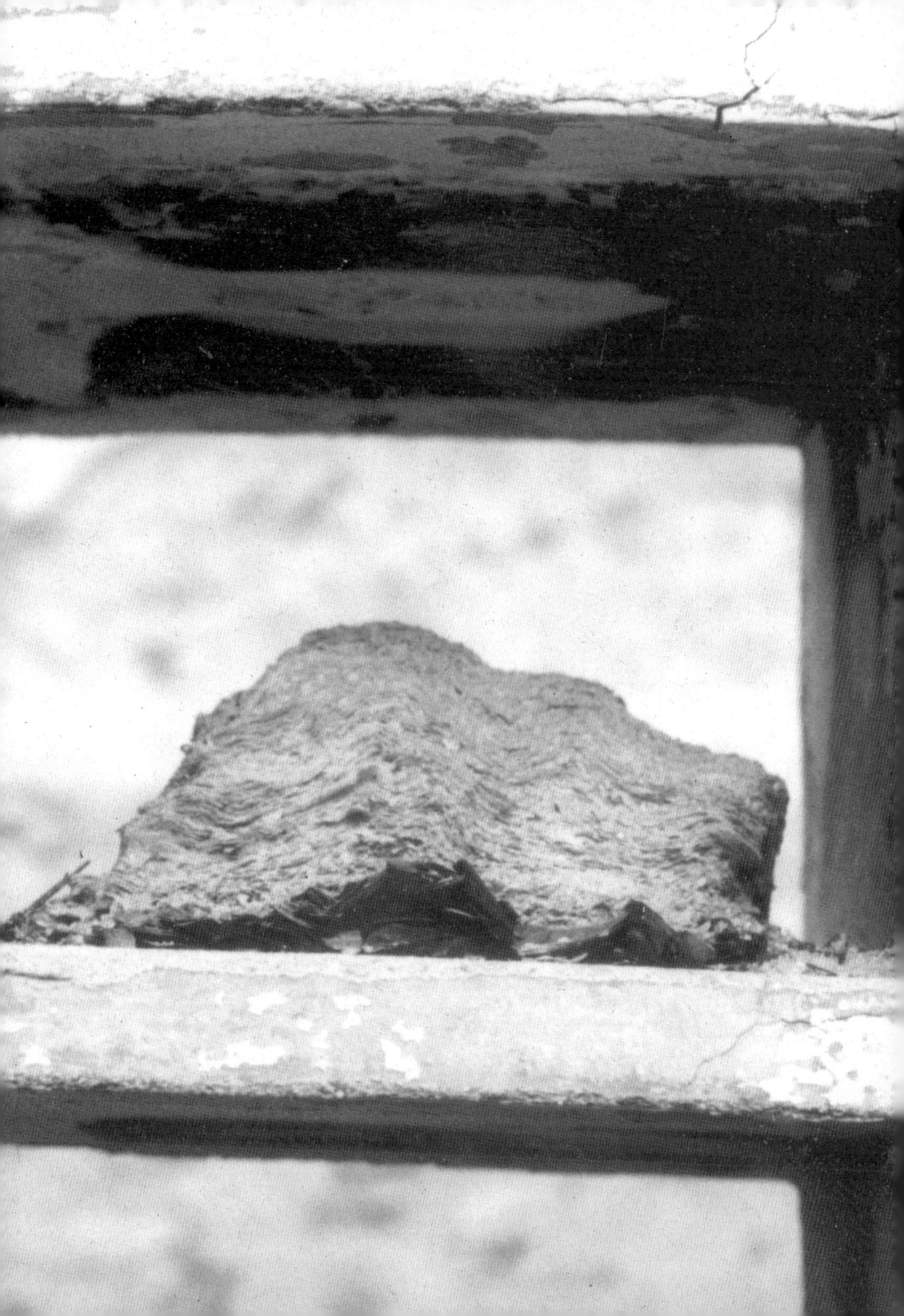

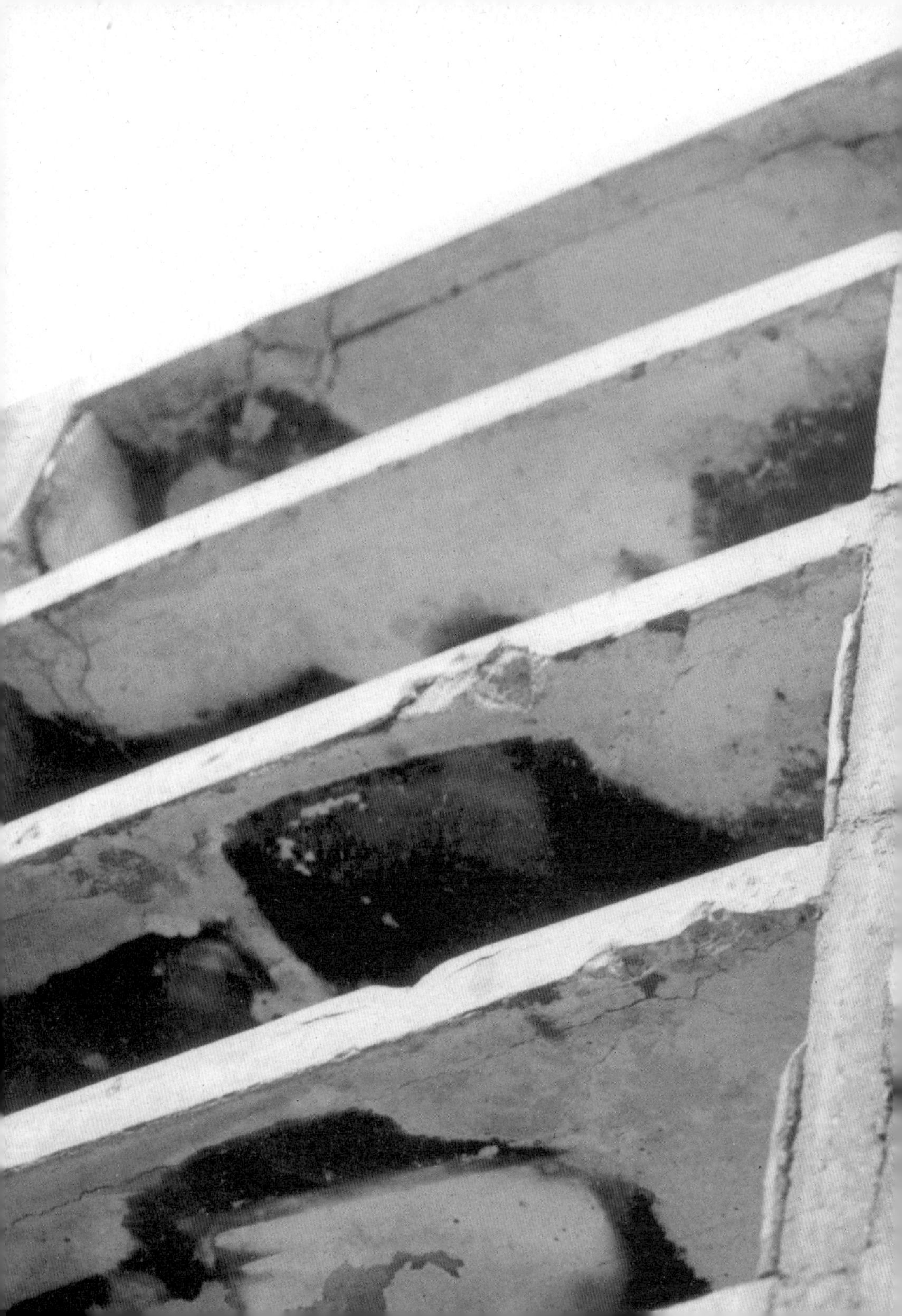

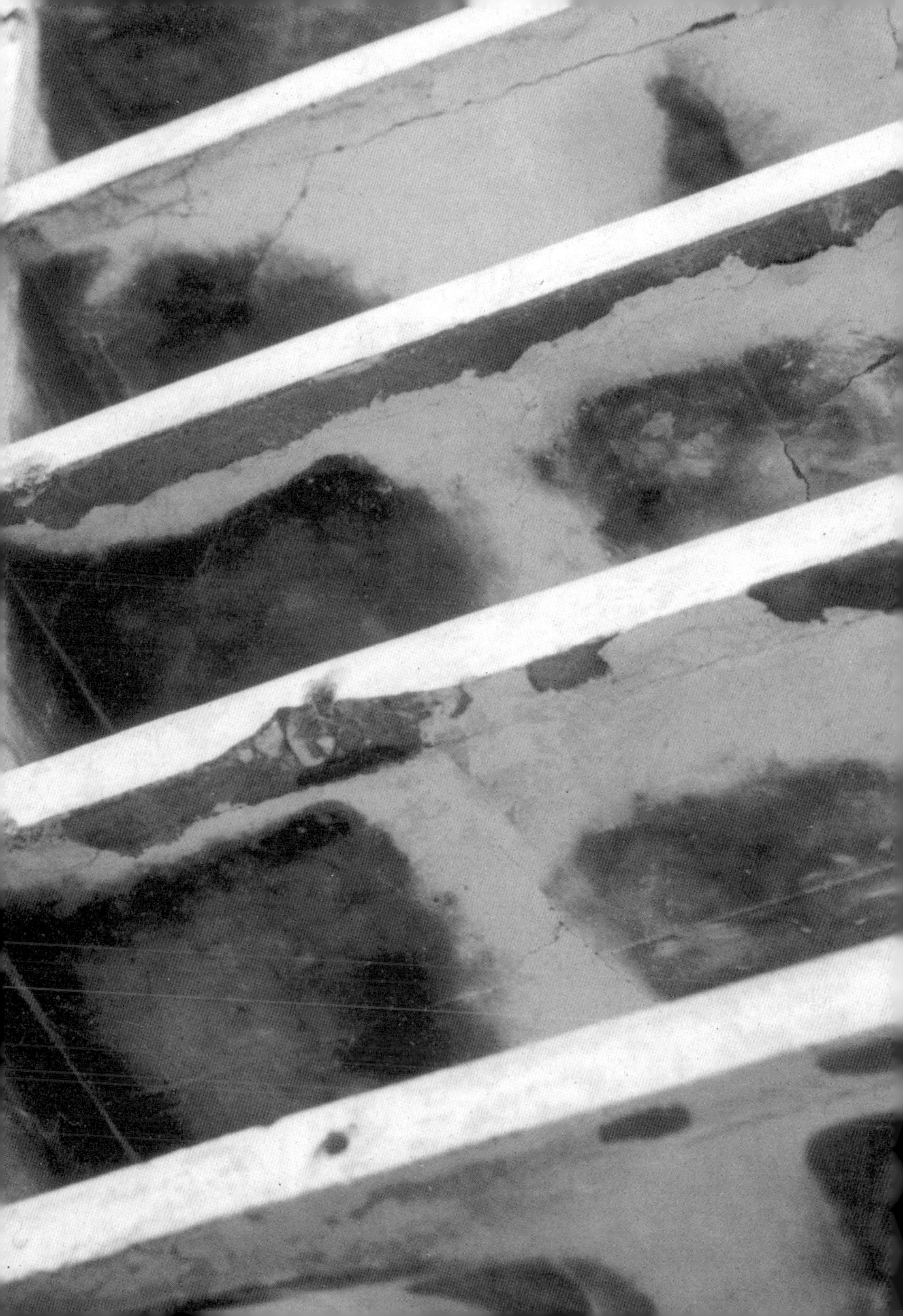

# *A Concise History of Australia*

STUART MACINTYRE

Litt[illegible]



# CAPITALISM, SOCIALISM OR BARBARISM? THE AUSTRALIAN PREDICAMENT

## Essays in Contemporary Political Economy

# THE OXFORD HISTORY OF AUSTRALIA

## VOLUME 4
## 1901–1942
## THE SUCCEEDING AGE

STUART MACINTYRE

Henry Reynolds

# The Other Side of the Frontier

*Aboriginal resistance to the European invasion of Australia*

Foreword by C. D. Rowley

Paul Carter

# LIVING IN A NEW COUNTRY

*History, travelling and language*

# My Place

# MAN ALONE

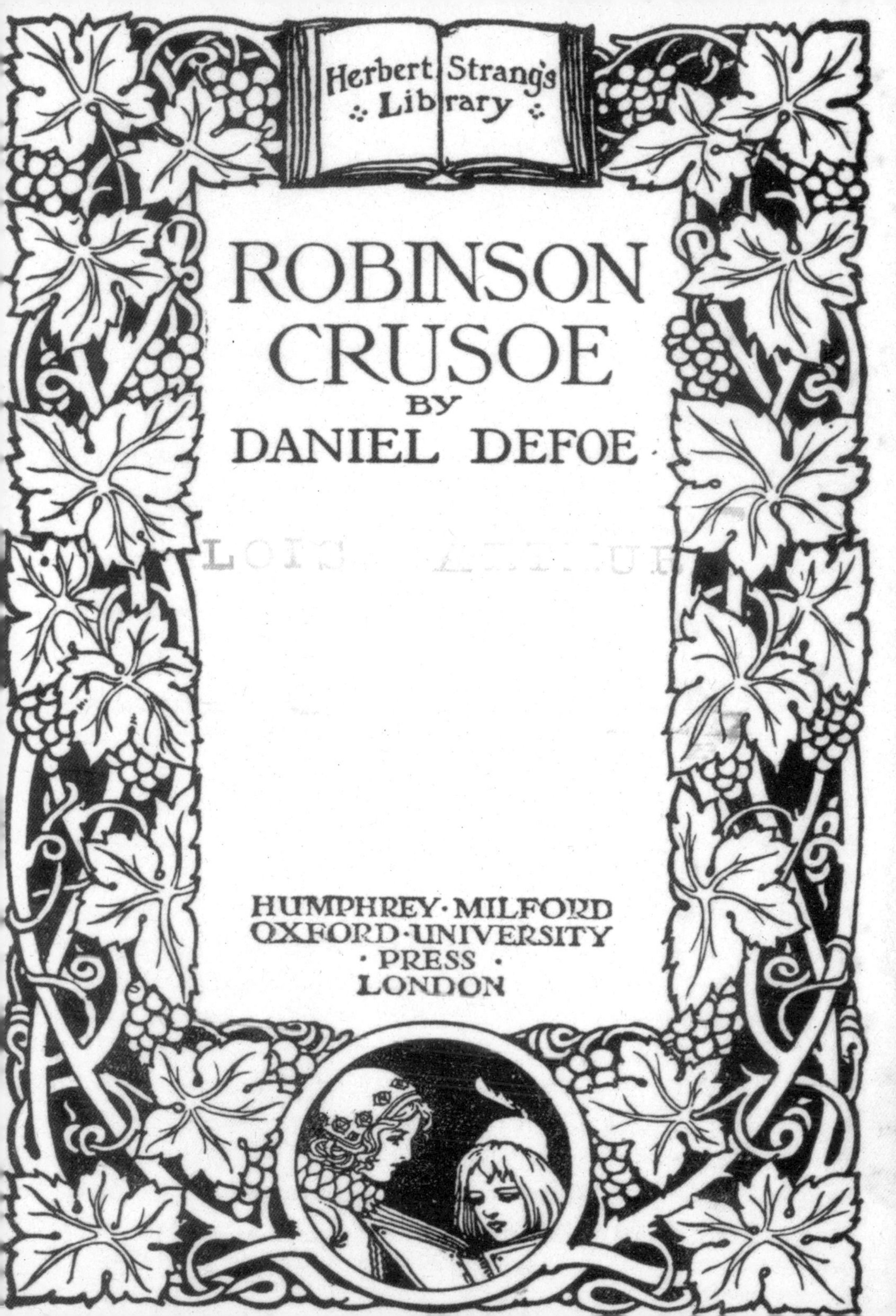


# ROBINSON CRUSOE

BY

DANIEL DEFOE

HUMPHREY · MILFORD
OXFORD · UNIVERSITY
· PRESS ·
LONDON

# Principles of Tourism

# Tourism

## An Introductory Text

Second Edition

Sharron Dickman

A.A.Eng., B.Sc., B.Admin., M.A., Ph.D., F.A.I.T.T., F.A.M.I.

Edward Arnold
A division of Hodder Headline
SYDNEY LONDON AUCKLAND

# Oriental Enlightenment

---

## The encounter between Asian and Western thought

J. J. Clarke

# Asia's Modern Century

New edition

# MARX AND THE THIRD WORLD

# V. I. Lenin

# Against Imperialist War

## Articles and Speeches

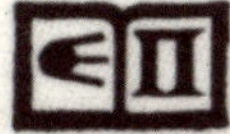

# INDONESIAN-ENGLISH
# ENGLISH-INDONESIAN
# DICTIONARY

John Pilger

# HIDDEN AGENDAS

# THE WAITER'S
## HANDBOOK

ACTIVE HISTORY

# THE GROWTH OF WESTERN CIVILISATION



Don Scott & Lindsay Dann

NELSON

# AN ASIAN TRAGEDY

## CONFLICT IN INDOCHINA

ALAN POLLOCK

MANAGEMENT
A Pacific Rim Focus

Dear ETSSC comrades,

# MAI KOLIA TETUN

with Love and Solidarity,

THE FREE TIMOR CAMPAIGN.

Dear ETSSC,

# MAI KOLIA TETUN

With love
and solidarity
The Free Timor
Campaign.

# Picking up the Pieces

# RETURNING TO NOTHING

## THE MEANING OF LOST PLACES

Peter Read

Department of History
Australian National University

Dear GFFTL

# MAI KOLIA TETUN

love and solidarity

THE FREE TIMOR CAMPAIGN

# STANDARD TETUM

---

# ENGLISH DICTIONARY

ninemsn Home | Hotmail | Community | Shopping | Web Search | Passport sign out

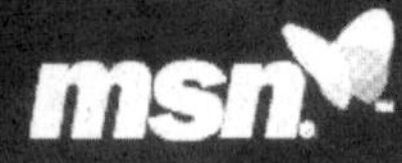

Hotmail® *tomjnicholson@hotmail.com*

Inbox | Compose | Address Book | Folders | Options | Messenger | Calendar | Help

**Folder: Inbox**

**From:** **Peter Mansell <pmansell@unimelb.edu.au>** Save Address - Block Sender
To: Tom Nicholson <tomjnicholson@hotmail.com> Save Address
**Subject: Re: book donations for East Timor**
Date: Fri, 19 Jan 2001 11:03:27 -0800

Reply | Reply All | Forward | Delete | Previous | Next | Close

Tom,
I will be around the office most of next week, so I am pretty flexible. How about early afternoon Monday (~2:00pm)? If that doesn't suit, then feel free to nominate a time/day that suits you better. Wednesday afternoon would be difficult for me.
Regards
Peter

At 09:18 PM 18-01-01 +1100, you wrote:

> Dear Peter
> Thanks for the email.
>
> I would be deligted to pick up the boxes at a time that suits you.
>
> I can make it any day of the week with a bit of notice. Please let me know what suits you.
>
> I hope all goes well with you.
>
> Warm regards
> Tom
>
>> From: Peter Mansell <pmansell@unimelb.edu.au>
>> To: Tom Nicholson <tomjnicholson@hotmail.com>
>> Subject: Re: book donations for East Timor
>> Date: Tue, 02 Jan 2001 11:32:10 -0800
>>
>> Dear Tom,
>> Sorry for taking so long to get back to you about the vet books I have for Timor. I think I have got a reasonable collection for you, covering a fairly broad range of veterinary topics. There are some older texts, but things that are still of value I think. I have boxed them all up and they are now sitting in my office awaiting your instructions. There are 7 sturd boxes, about 90kg in total. Drop me a line when you are ready to arrange the next step.
>> Hope you had a good Christmas.
>> Peter
>>
>> At 07:08 AM 29-11-00 +0000, you wrote:
>>
>>> Dear Peter
>>> Thanks for the email.
>>> In reply to your question about choosiness: I have simply been using my judgement on whether a book will be useful. I think it is worth being discriminating, mainly because it is quite costly to actually send mate over to East Timor, and also time-consuming for the librarians to proce the material they are given. If the books are in a field in which you some knowledge, I would suggest that you use your judgement in determin how useful the books might be to a fledgling university library. That much of an answer, I know.

In terms of subject matter, I understood from Judy that the texts you h
are agricultural and vet. So long as they are relatively up-to-date an
relevant to a tropical climate, these are prized. Dictionaries and ESL
texts are enormously valuable. Likewise politics and engineering.

Please let me know when it would suit you for me to collect the books,
how I can help in any other way.
Warm regards, and thanks
Tom

>From: Peter Mansell <pmansell@unimelb.edu.au>
>To: Tom Nicholson <tomjnicholson@hotmail.com>
>Subject: Re: book donations for East Timor
>Date: Mon, 27 Nov 2000 14:42:41 +1100
>
>Dear Tom,
>Thanks for your reply. Are you choosey about what type of book you
want, or
>how recent an edition they are, or are you open to any and all
donations? I
>have several boxes of books from the deceased estate of a colleague
>(nothing more recent than 5 years old, and some substantially older),
>well as an assortment that I have procured from various other sources.
>you can give me an idea of what you are interested in, then I will get
the
>boxes together and tell you how much I have for you.
>Regards
>Peter
>
>At 17:20 19/11/2000 -0500, you wrote:
> >Dear Peter
> >
> >Judy Blood gave me your email adress and suggested I get in contact
>you
> >in relation to some veterinary and agriculture texts that you might
> >prepared to donate to the University Library in East Timor.
> >
> >I have been co-ordinating the collection and trasportation of variou
> >donated texts, recently mostly agriculture and veterinary, for the U
> >Library and would be happy to collect any material that you are prep
>to
> >donate.
> >
> >I can be comtacted at this hotmail address or on 9329 0709, or 9481
0544.
> >
> >Warm regards
> >
> >Tom Nicholson
> >
> >
> >________________________________________________________________
> >Get Your Private, Free E-mail from MSN Hotmail at
http://www.hotmail.com.
> >
> >Share information about yourself, create your own public profile at
> >http://profiles.msn.com.
> >
>Peter Mansell BVSc PhD MACVSc
>University of Melbourne
>250 Princes Highway
>Werribee, Victoria 3030
>PLEASE NOTE CHANGE >> pmansell@unimelb.edu.au
>Ph: 03 9731 2222, Fax: 03 9731 2366

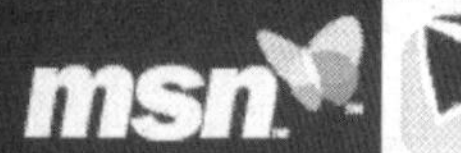


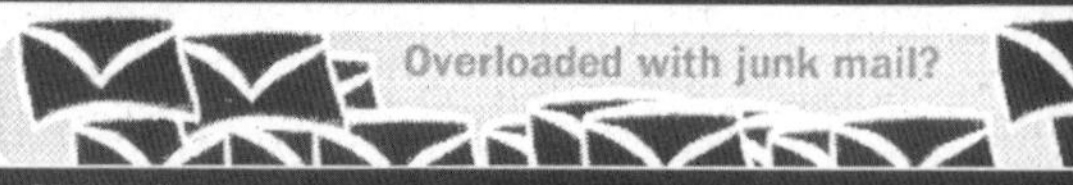


Hotmail® *tomjnicholson@hotmail.com*

**Inbox**

**From:** "Daniel Nicholson" <danielpn@enternet.com.au> Save Address - Block Sender
**To:** <danielpn@enternet.com.au> Save Address
**Subject:** One year commerorations in East Timor, Maliana: Verbal diarrhoea of an observer part 302.
**Date:** Tue, 5 Sep 2000 08:57:58 +1000

Dear all,

Tonight, one year ago, Dili burned. September 4th was the Saturday after the ballot. The news footage focused on the Hotel Mahkota, where all the journos were staying. Two militia men attacked that day, in front of 50 police or more. One fired one shot through the front window. The journos ran up the stairs and booked their flights out. That night, the big fires in Dili began. The journalists, leaving next morning, sat on the roof and drank themselves silly. They didn't even bother to film. After they left, the real destruction began.

One year ago tonight the university was burnt. The education campus, including the English library where several student leaders worked, was absolutely destroyed. No room has a roof. The main campus had a bomb put in the front. The ground floor was pretty badly burnt. The students gathered in front of the campus this evening. They put candles all down the street. They covered the roof of the university entrance with about fifty candles, and wrote solidaritas - solidarity - in candles.

All over Dili people lined the streets with candles. The whole city was lit up with candles. Along the road to our house, the local youth burned tires - it was eerie. Where people fell, there were piles of candles and sometimes flowers. People stood by the side of the roads everywhere, and watched the candles burn. When cars drove past, they told them to slow down. A whole city commemorated, with fire, the day their houses and lives were engulfed by it.

We all went to the one year anniversary of the ballot on the 30th of August. I saw Alexander Downer lay his wreath at Santa Cruz, I heard his words. I saw the speeches by big men out the front of the big UN building. But what I saw tonight, real people commemorating their real experience - silently - was worth one thousand hypocritical wreaths from Australian politicians. Even the Yothu Yindi concert on the 30th, which we went to, wasn't like I expected.

Maybe people aren't ready to celebrate yet. When you ask people where they were one year ago today, you understand why. Antero was in the Hotel Turismo. He didn't leave his room for a week. Lindo was near his village. The whole village went to the forest. And these were two of the lucky people. Antero ended up in Darwin, on the last evacuation flight. Lindo's village only had the military headquarters burnt, the other five villages in his sub-district were destroyed.

***

Kate and I went to Maliana on Saturday. Maliana is in the west of East Timor, near the border with Indonesia. It was one of the worst affected last year by militia and military violence, and is one of the areas where there are still big militia problems.

To get there, we went west along the north coast. The road is like it is all along the north coast: narrow, winding it's way around the cliffs, sometimes dropping away a hundred feet to the sea, and breathtakingly spectacular. We drove along it until we reached Batugade, which is right on the Indonesian border. Batugade was the first town Indonesia took in October 1975. Last year, as one the last places they left, it was devastated. The UN operates out of temporary buildings, and Australian tanks rattle around the streets. Even the troop carriers have machine gunners mounted on the top.

From Batugade, we headed south and into the hills. We climbed until we reached Balibo, where five Australian journalists were infamously killed on October 16 1975. All along here, the road is quite close to the border. On the western side are forests, where the militias now wander. The Australians are responsible for security here, so we passed armoured cars and checkpoints and bases along the way. We even saw two Australian foot patrols, complete with painted faces, who had evidently been out hunting militia.

From Balibo we descended until we reached the end of the hills. We crossed a river to an Australian checkpoint, where we all got out of the bus, had our bags searched and were checked with an airport-style metal detector. This was the checkpoint that had a couple of grenades lobbed into it a few months ago. Its only a few hundred metres from the border, and completely exposed. They told us they had thermal imaging now, so they didn't have too many problems.

From there, we crossed a broad plain. Maliana district is the biggest gricultural producer in East Timor. However, this year the rice paddies ere uncultivated. We passed a ruined transmigration community. This plain ad been mostly cultivated by Indonesian transmigrants, but now they had eturned home, and the fields were left bare.

aliana is on the very edge of this plain, just under another set of hills. ne town is very spectacular, partly built on the plain and aprtly in the ills. We were there for a reconciliation meeting. That morning, on of the udent leaders' partner had his first child. He named it Reconciliano. The eeting was attended by about fifty people. The speakers included Falintil eader Falur, Aderito, the head of the East Timor jurists association, and thers. It was great to see the students, especially in Maliana, grappling ith the big issues.

**

ne day we were in Maliana was one year since what they called "the tragedy f September 2nd". That day, the people confronted the militia in the middle f Maliana. They stoned the militia, the militia stoned them back. Then the ilitary or police opened fire. Five people were killed. This story was not nusual. The same thing happened in Dili, Viqueque and other places. Because alintil didn't fight, people think, and it is generally reported, that the opulation were passive towards the militia and military. Actually, the urden of militant resistance fell to the youth and students; and they esisted effectively, but at great human cost. The loss of life last year ould have been much greater if it weren't for these groups, who in many laces, like Santa Cruz where the students were, controlled the eighbourhoods until the people fled to churches or the mountains.

nat night, we went to the family ceremony for three of the five killed. nere were about a hundred people there, including the local UN staff. We ent into the house, where photos of the men sat, along with flowers, andles and one of each of their shirts. The families sat there crying. ater, the Timorese crowded into the house and prayed for the dead souls. ne distinctive mourning song rang out across the garden (God hear us rying), along with the wails of the widows. It was clear that the pain and adness of last year were still being felt strongly felt by these people. utside, two Australian tanks passed. The fear, too, was still there.

o wonder the celebrations of August 30th felt a bit strange...

ove to all

eel free to write to me...

an

S - Traditional Timorese saying: "A year when Essendon wins the flag is a ood year to be overseas."

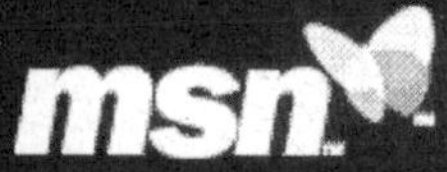

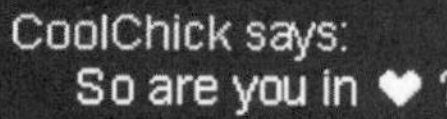

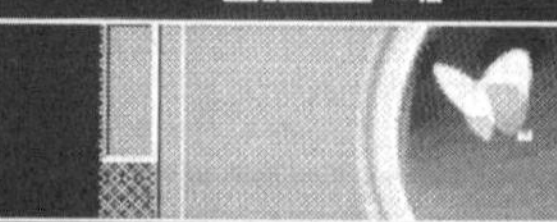

**Hotmail®** *tomjnicholson@hotmail.com*

## Folder:Inbox

**From:** **Sarah Barnard <sbarnard@kangan.edu.au>** Save Address - Block Sender
To: 'Tom Nicholson' <tomjnicholson@hotmail.com> Save Address
CC: Paulina Reinoga <preinoga@kangan.edu.au> Save Address
**Subject:** **RE: More books for East Timor**
Date: Mon, 29 Jan 2001 07:55:58 +1100

Hi Tom,

Glad you're interested about the books. The library here will be open on Mon, Tue and Thurs from 10.00 - 2.00pm. The librarian working here is Paulina Reinoga. I'll let her know where the books are - they are in a huge pile with East Timor written all over them, so it shouldn't be a problem!

Maybe give her a ring when you want to come over. The books are in the old library - the new (much smaller) library is right opposite reception in Building A. Paulina will be able to open up the old library for you so you can pack it all into your car like last time. There are approximately 40 boxes - you might need to make two trips.

Any way, any probs let me know. Phone number here is 9318 2488. Paulina's email is preinoga@kangan.edu.au. My phone number at Broady is 9279 2428.

Cheers

Sarah

> -----Original Message-----
> From: Tom Nicholson [SMTP:tomjnicholson@hotmail.com]
> Sent: Thursday, January 18, 2001 9:03 PM
> To: sbarnard@kangan.edu.au
> Subject: Re: More books for East Timor
>
> Dear Sarah
>
> I just sent you an email, but the computer crashed simultaneously, so I am
>
> not sure if it got through. If not...
>
> Thanks for the email and for continuing to collect the books.
>
> Sorry it has taken me a while to get back to you. I have been away for
> while without easy email access.
>
> I would be delighted to come and pick up the boxes of books at a time tat
> suits you, or the new/relevant librarian.
>
> Please let me know when that would be.
>
> Warm regards, and thanks
>
> Tom
>
>
> >From: Sarah Barnard <sbarnard@kangan.edu.au>
> >To: "'tomjnicholson@hotmail.com'" <tomjnicholson@hotmail.com>
> >Subject: More books for East Timor
> >Date: Tue, 19 Dec 2000 14:12:00 +1100
> >
> >Hi Tom,
> >
> >I have some more books and magazines for East Timor - so far about 18
> >boxes.

>I think I will have at least another 5-7 by the time I'm finished too.
I'm
>on leave as of this Friday (22/12/00) and won't actually be returning to
>Avondale. I will be based at Broadmeadows next year - and won't start
there
>until January 29, 2001.
>
>I have stacked up the boxes of books for you in the library. If you were
to
>let me know when you wanted to come and get them, I could get one of the
>girls from reception to let you into the library to collect them.
>
>As of January 29, 2001 the new librarian will start work at Avondale, but
>she will be based in a smaller room near reception (we have had to close
up
>the old room where the library was). So, I guess she could show where
they
>are - I can certainly let her know the details etc.
>
>Hope at least a small part of this makes sense to you! Let me know what
>your
>plan of attack will be.
>
>All the best for Christmas! Thanks very much for the letter you sent - it
>has been a real pleasure to help you with your work.
>
>Cheers
>
>Sarah
>
>Sarah Barnard
>Campus Librarian
>Learning Resource Centre
>
>Kangan Batman TAFE
>Avondale Heights Campus
>Ph: 9318-2488
>sbarnard@kangan.edu.au
>
>
>Sarah Barnard
>Campus Librarian
>Learning Resource Centre
>
>Kangan Batman TAFE
>Avondale Heights Campus
>Ph: 9318-2488
>sbarnard@kangan.edu.au
>

---

# *Natural Selection*

CHARLES DARWIN

RICHARD DAWKINS

# THE BLIND WATCHMAKER

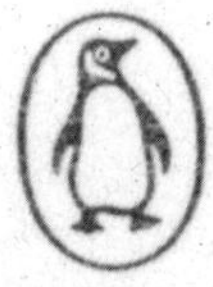

PENGUIN BOOKS

# Revolution

# The Bible ✠ Story

*The spirit of man is the candle of the Lord, lit by God and pointing to God; and he who fights against reason, fights against God.*

BENJAMIN WHICHCOTE
Provost of King's College, Cambridge, 1645–60

PELICAN BOOKS

A23

# RELIGION AND THE RISE OF CAPITALISM

BY R. H. TAWNEY

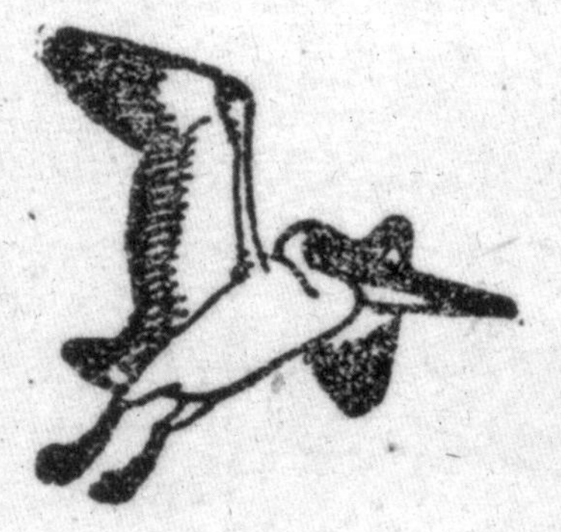

# DEATH OF A SALESMAN

ARTHUR MILLER

Anthony Giddens

---

# THE THIRD WAY

## The Renewal of Social Democracy

*The Portable*

# KARL MARX

*Selected, translated in part,*
*and with an Introduction by*
*Eugene Kamenka*

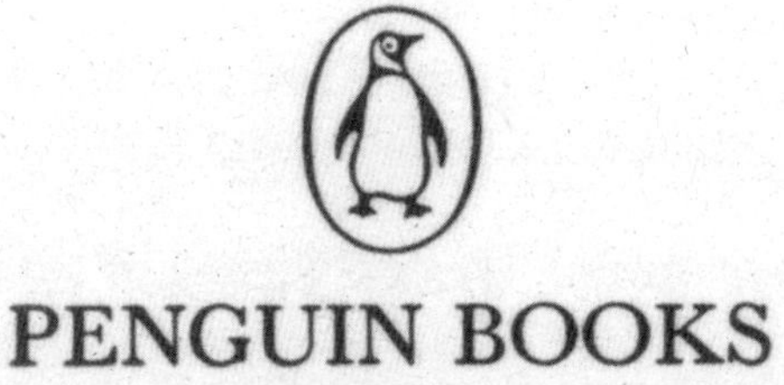

PENGUIN BOOKS

# *Australian Economics Dictionary*

## FOR STUDENTS

John Becroft

*Penguin Reference Books*

# The Penguin Macquarie Dictionary of Economics & Finance

GEORGE ORWELL

---

# *Homage to Catalonia*

AND

LOOKING BACK ON THE SPANISH WAR

PENGUIN BOOKS

WORKERS OF ALL COUNTRIES, UNITE!

V. I. LENIN

# WHAT IS TO BE DONE?

## BURNING QUESTIONS OF OUR MOVEMENT[1]

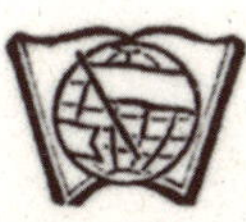

FOREIGN LANGUAGES PUBLISHING HOUSE
Moscow 1951

# CONSUMER BEHAVIOR

# CONSUMER BEHAVIOR

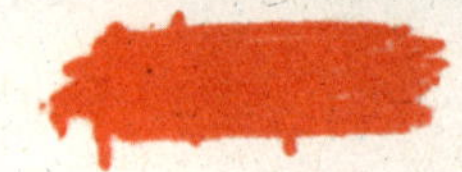

# *Mao Tse-tung*

## An Anthology of His Writing

EDITED WITH AN INTRODUCTION BY
ANNE FREMANTLE

KARL MARX
FREDERICK ENGELS

# MANIFESTO OF THE COMMUNIST PARTY

FOREIGN LANGUAGES PRESS
PEKING 1970

NAME
SUBJEC
CL
YEAR

# Space to Dream

# Permanent Red

ALDOUS HUXLEY

# Brave New World

**A TRIAD GRAFTON BOOK**
A Division of the Collins Publishing Group

**Aldous Huxley**

# Brave New World

SIMONE DE BEAUVOIR

# A Very Easy Death

*Translated by Patrick O'Brian*

2

PENGUIN BOOKS

SIMONE
DE BEAUVOIR

# The Second Sex

*Translated and Edited by*
H. M. Parshley

*Germaine Greer*

# Female Eunuch

Naomi Wolf

# THE BEAUTY MYTH

## How Images of Beauty Are Used Against Women

# The Fontana Dictionary of Modern Thought

# I BELIEVE

## NINETEEN PERSONAL PHILOSOPHIES

LONDON · UNWIN BOOKS

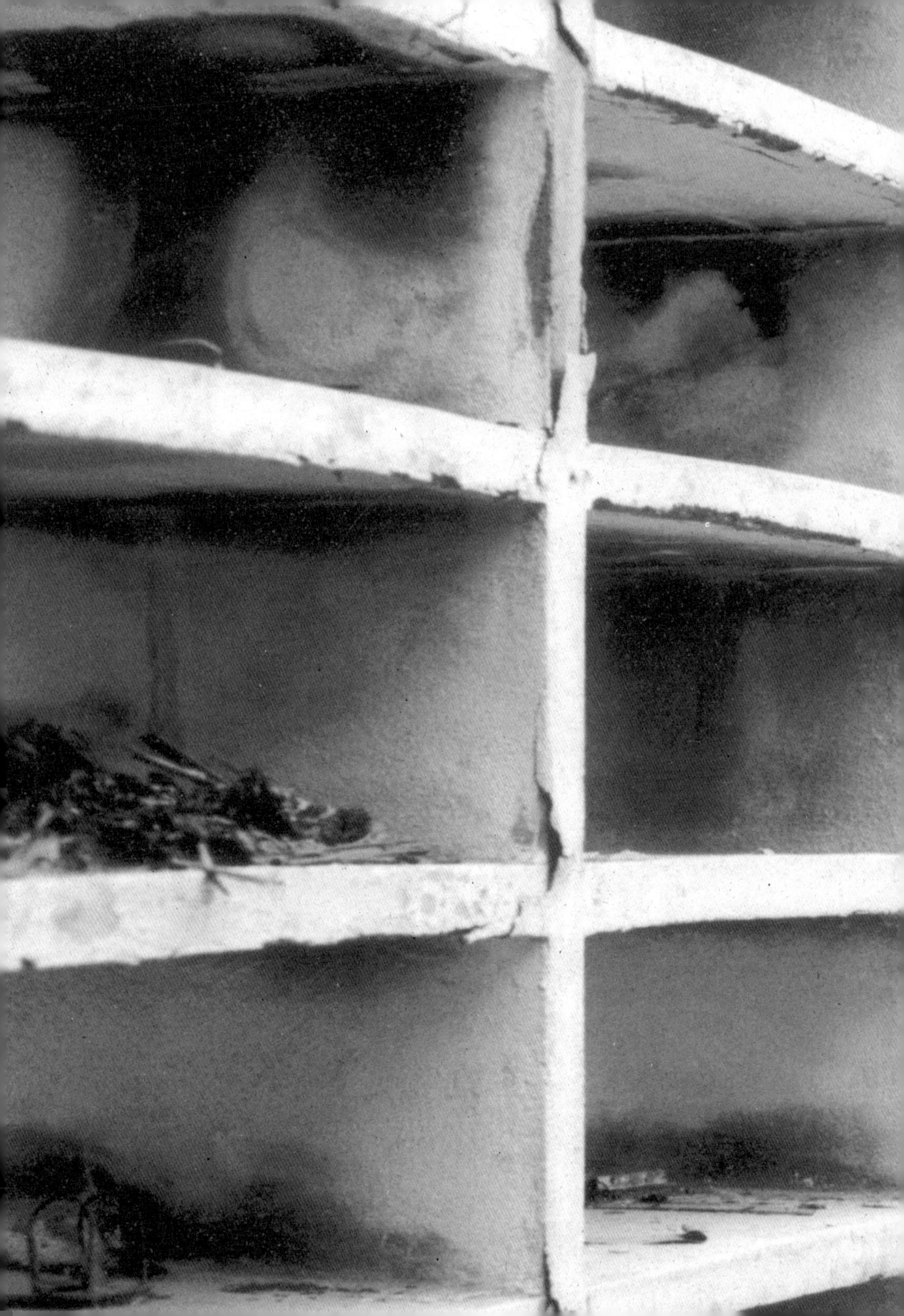

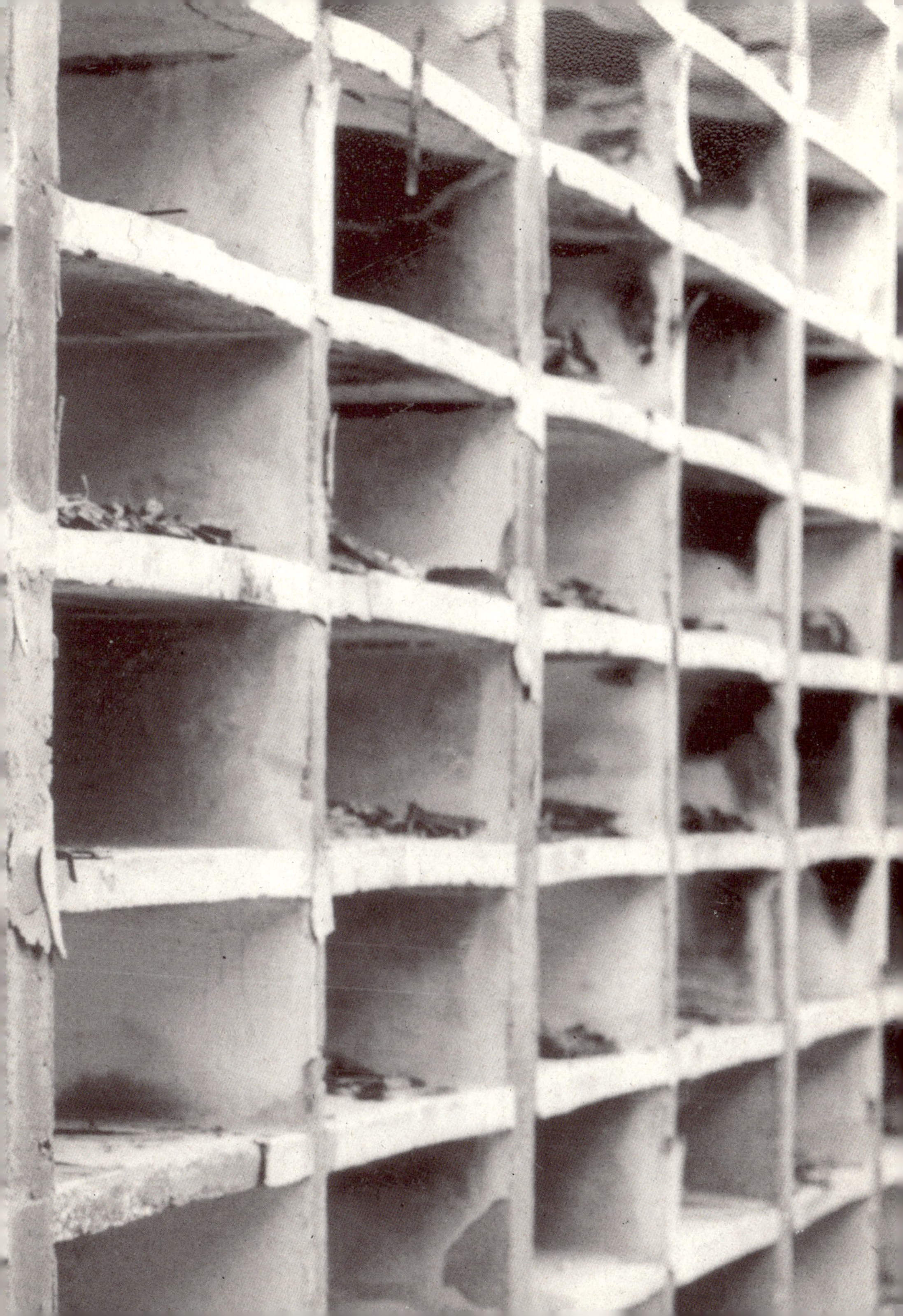

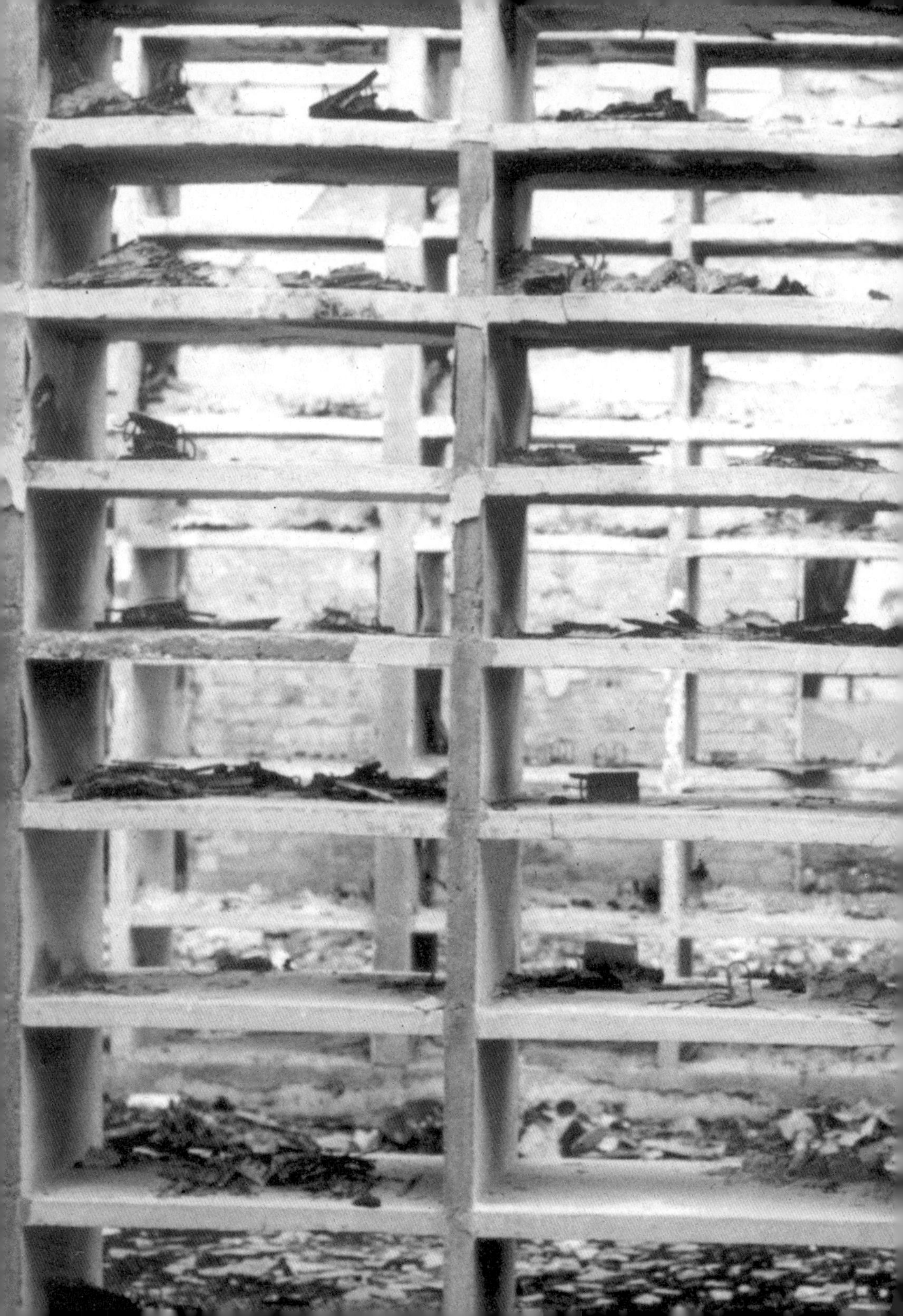

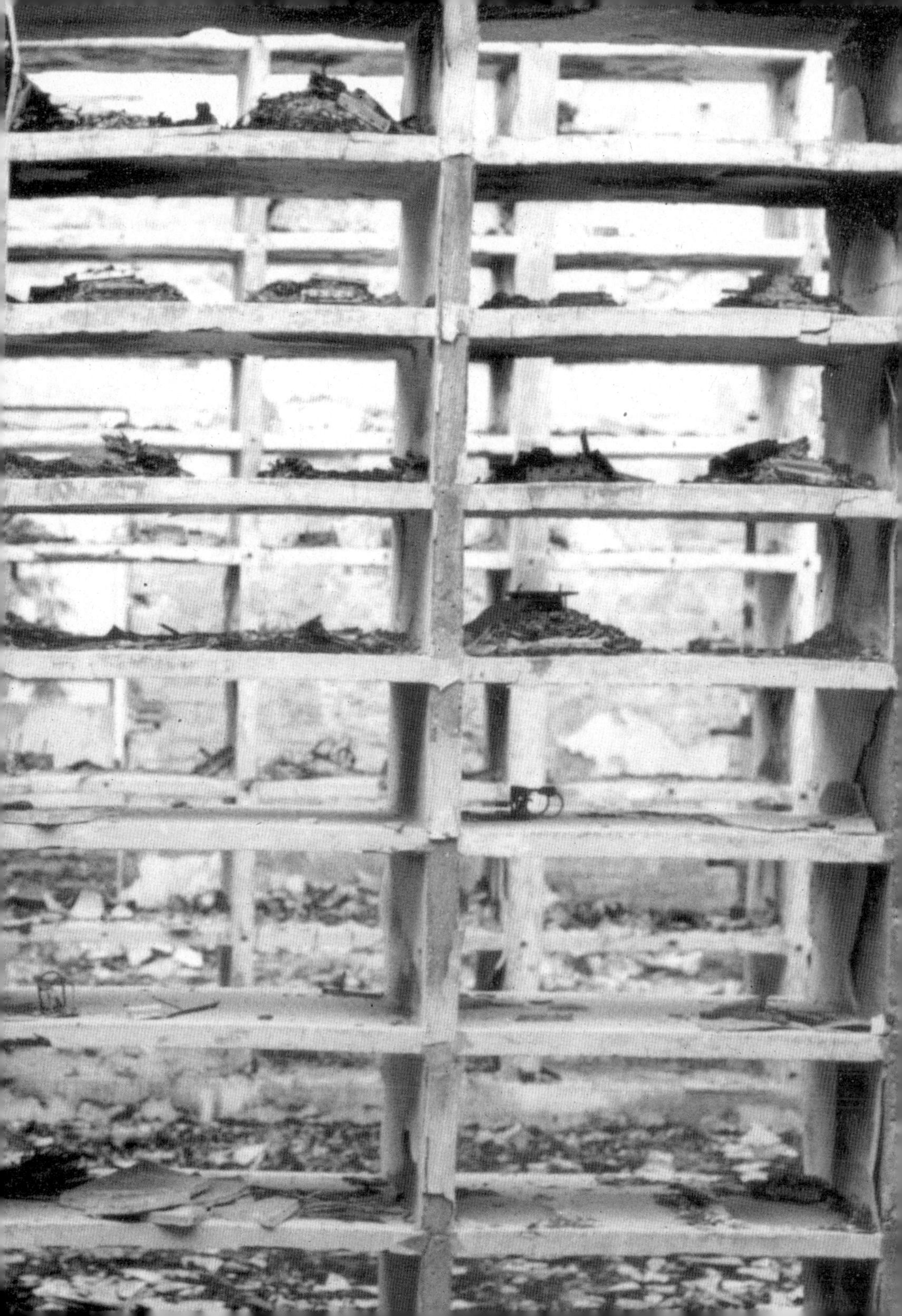

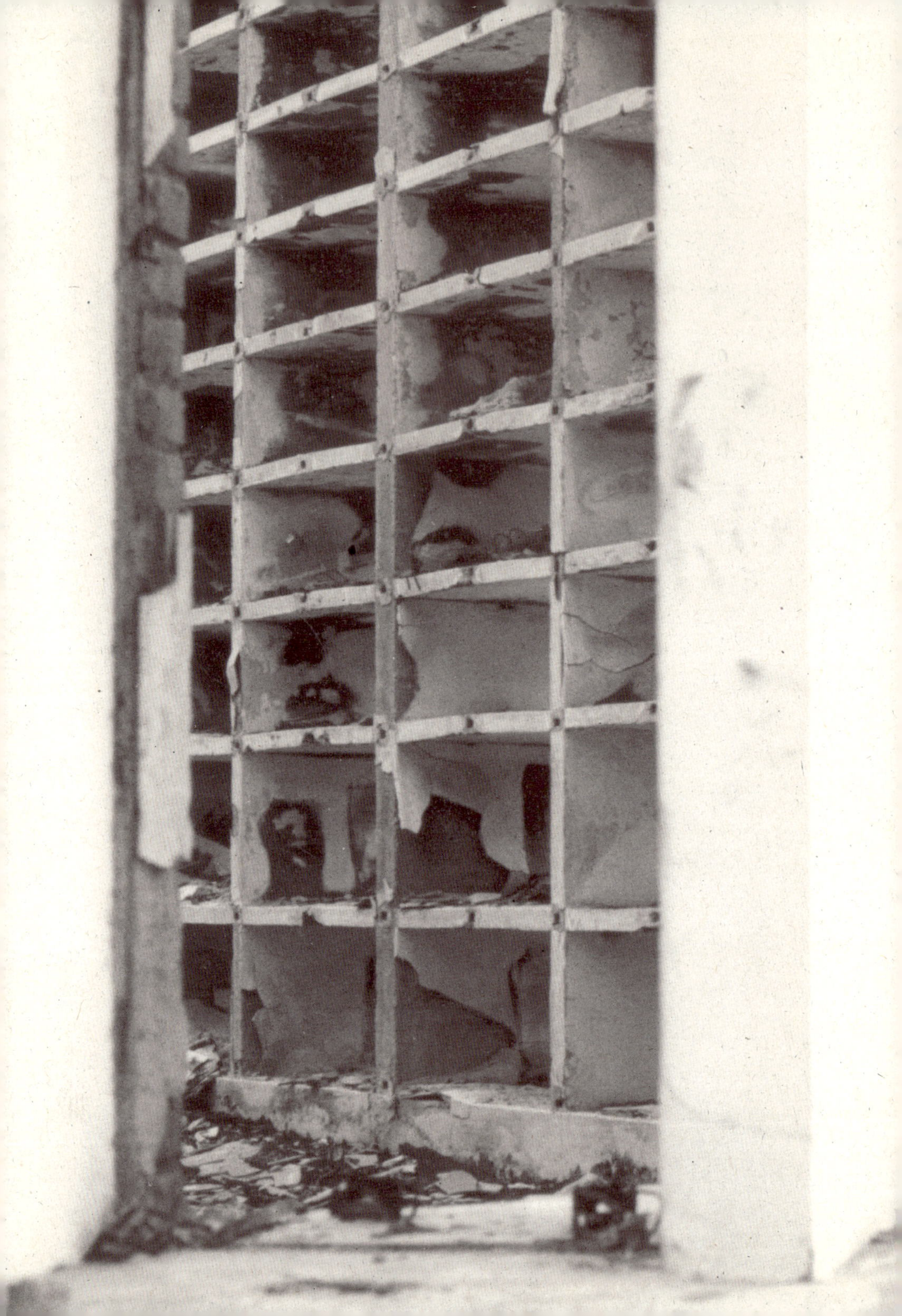

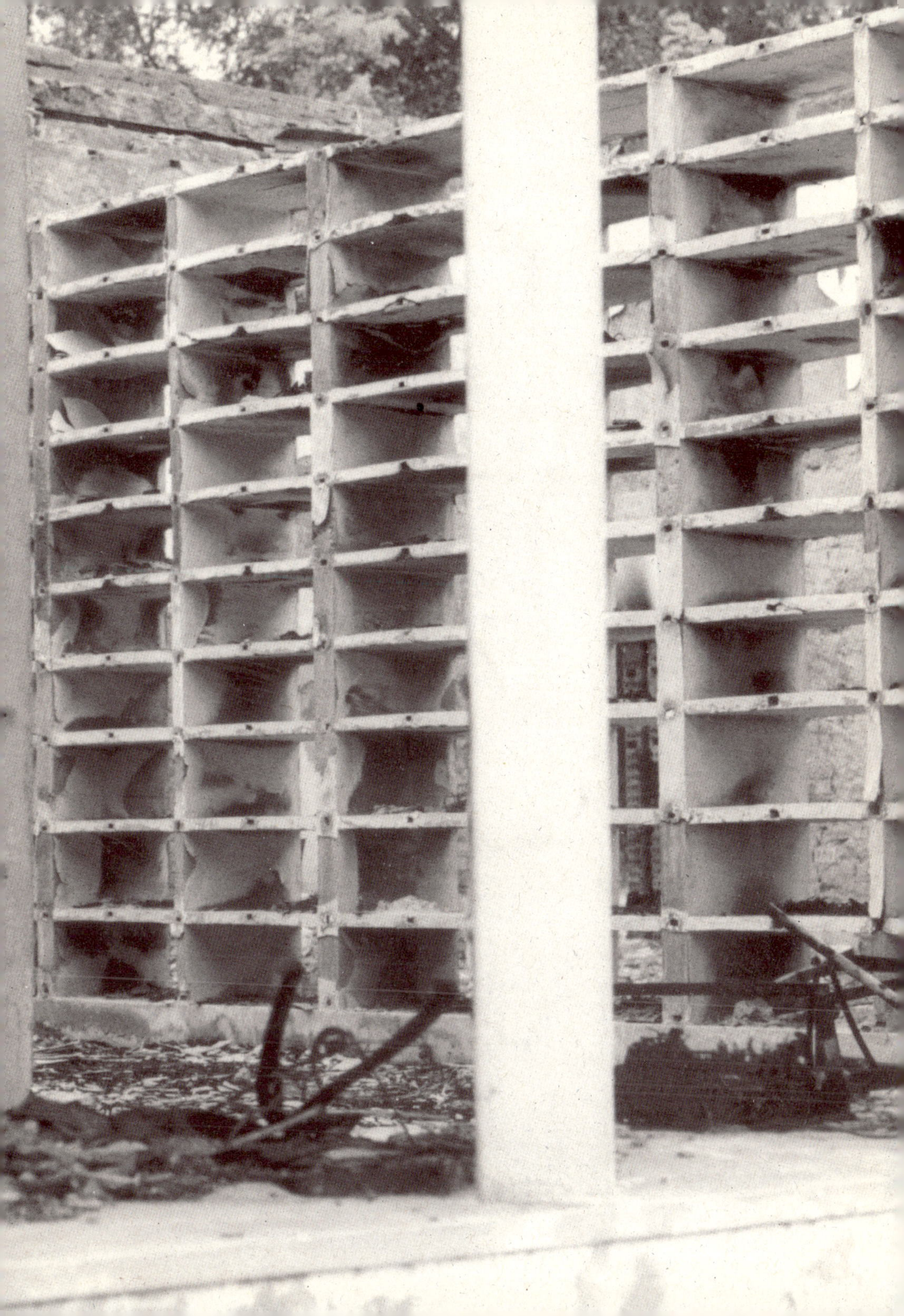

This book is dedicated to<br>
the unknown victims of<br>
Hiroshima and Nagasaki,<br>
the people of Korea,<br>
40 000 of whom were murdered<br>
by the United States<br>
bomb tests and the<br>
66 560 000 others<br>
who are today facing the<br>
re-escalation of a<br>
war which has already claimed<br>
the lives of 3 000 000

and to all people<br>
murdered, maimed,<br>
starved, used,<br>
robbed and<br>
kept in poverty<br>
by<br>
the masters of war

# One thousand years of drawing

a studio vista | dutton pictureback

# Man and His Symbols

**Carl G. Jung** and M. -L. von Franz Joseph L. Henderson
Jolande Jacobi Aniela Jaffé

Roland Barthes

# MYTHOLOGIES

SELECTED AND TRANSLATED FROM THE FRENCH BY

Annette Lavers

V

Ann Beattie

# PICTURING WILL

VINTAGE

Joseph Heller

# PICTURE THIS

# I WILL

A DIARY OF

# BEAR

THE NAZI YEARS

# WITNESS

1933—1941

VICTOR KLEMPERER

Translated by Martin Chalmers

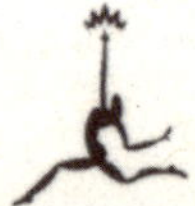

Elie Wiesel

# NIGHT

oreword by François Mauriac

Translated from the French by Stella Rodway

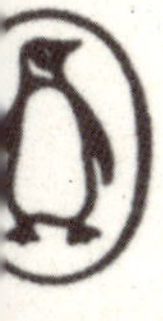

Penguin Books

# NO MEMORIAL

# GOYA

Goya 1

# *LUTHERAN LETTERS*

## Pier Paolo Pasolini

*Translated from the Italian by* STUART HOOD

CARCANET NEW PRESS / MANCHESTER
RAVEN ARTS PRESS / DUBLIN

PIER PAOLO PASOLINI

# SELECTED POEMS

# *Understanding Media*

The Extensions of Man, by

MARSHALL McLUHAN

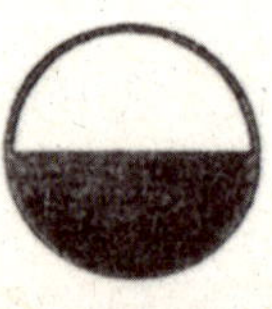

SPHERE BOOKS LIMITED LONDON

RICHARD WOLLHEIM

# *Art and its Objects*

PENGUIN BOOKS

REACH OUT

[redacted]

[redacted]

# Reaching Out

# DÜRER

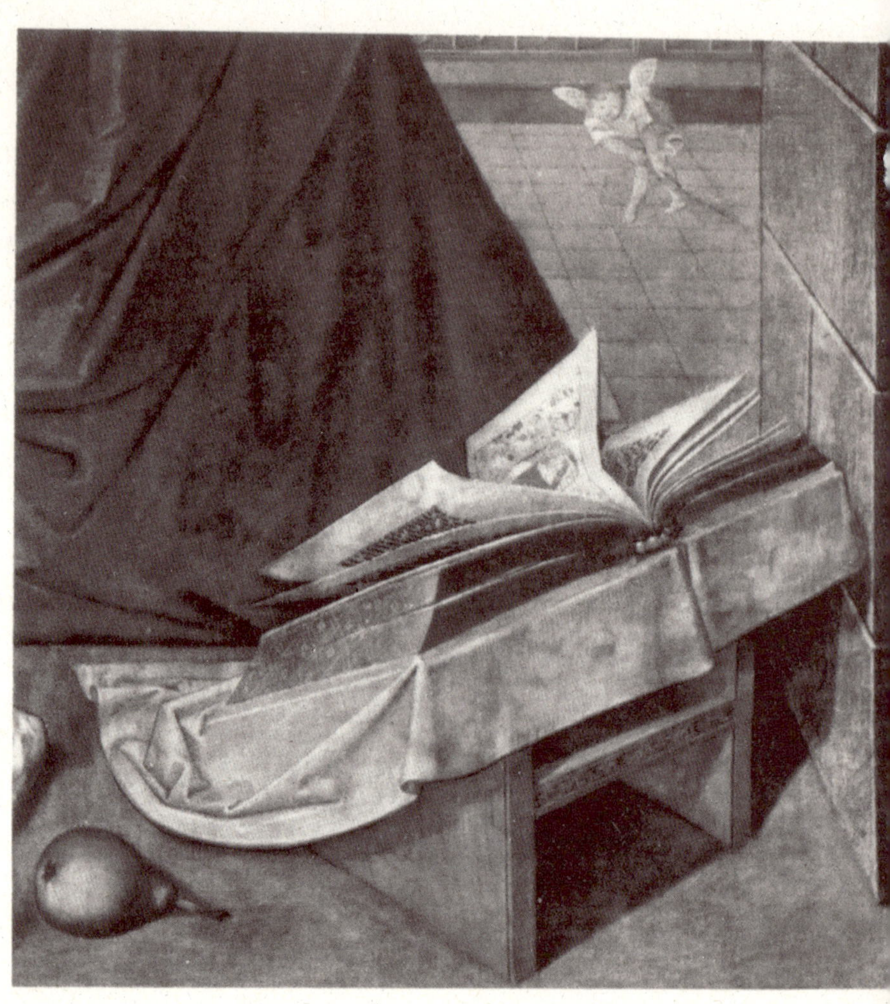